Every life should have a story worth retelling.

Reflections
In a Sailor's Eyes

Jack Binder, master mariner and ship's engineer,
with his wife Judith, homebuilt *Banyandah* in Sydney, Australia.
Launched in 1973, a year later with their two infant sons
they embarked on a magical life encircling Earth in ever-increasing circles
taking thirteen years to visit more than eighty countries.
In 2007, Jack and Jude, then grandparents married forty years,
circumnavigated Australia aboard that very same craft.
Back on dry land in 2009 they wrote
Two's a Crew detailing that adventurous journey.
Then after exploring Australia's southern shores, Jack wrote, *Where Wilds Winds Blow*.
A published writer since 1980, Cap'n Jack's articles often appear in periodicals.

This is dedicated to our grandchildren,
all ten of them and to another four connected to us
by the love and fun we share.
The future belongs to you, the events in this book shows
there is fun, knowledge and adventure awaiting you.

"Twenty years from now you will be more disappointed by the things that you didn't do than by the ones you did do. So throw off the bowlines. Sail away from the safe harbor. Catch the trade winds in your sails. Explore. Dream. Discover." ~ Mark Twain

Reflections in a Sailor's Eyes

An odyssey lasting far longer than ever imagined
by
Jack and Jude Binder

Tujays Publishing
Empire Vale P.O. NSW
Australia 2478
Email: capjack2j@gmail.com
Web: www.jackandjude.com

Copyright © Jack Binder 2015 - 2020

All photographs and diagrams by Jack and Judith Binder

All rights reserved. No part of this book may be reproduced or transmitted in any form or by any means electronic or mechanical, including photocopying, recording or by any information storage and retrieval system, without prior permission in writing from the publishers or authors.

First published in Australia 2015
Second Edition 2020

Papers used in the production of this book are natural, renewable and recyclable products sourced from sustainable

Note: Both imperial and metric measurements used throughout.
1 nautical mile (NM) = 1.15 land miles = 1.85 kilometres (km)
1 fathom = 6 feet = 1.83 metres (m)
Australian dollars are shown
Australian spelling is used

Binder, Jack, 1944 - .
    Reflections in a Sailor's Eyes / by Jack Binder;
    photographs by Judith Binder;
    edited by Judith Binder.
    ISBN 9780980872064 (pbk.)

    Other books by Jack Binder:
    Two's a Crew – ISBN 9780980872019
    Where Wild Winds Blow – ISBN 9780980872033
    Around the World in Ever Increasing Circles – ISBN 9780980872088

Reflections in a Sailor's Eyes

**"Every time it got hard, every time I got afraid
I just called to my love and got strength to go on."**

African Honeymoon	9
Failed Again	49
Banyandah	53
Running Scared at Spratly	57
The Dead Don't Cry	63
Maybe the World is Growing Smaller	75
Malpelo Lessons	81
Henry's Boo-Boo	121
To the Navel of the World	127
The One that Got Away	147
Rhumb Lines Around Australia	153
Fishing for Monsters	161
The People You Meet	165
Late Night Visitor	169
Moonlight Across the Southern Ocean	173
The Fall of Nan Jude	181
Glossary	189

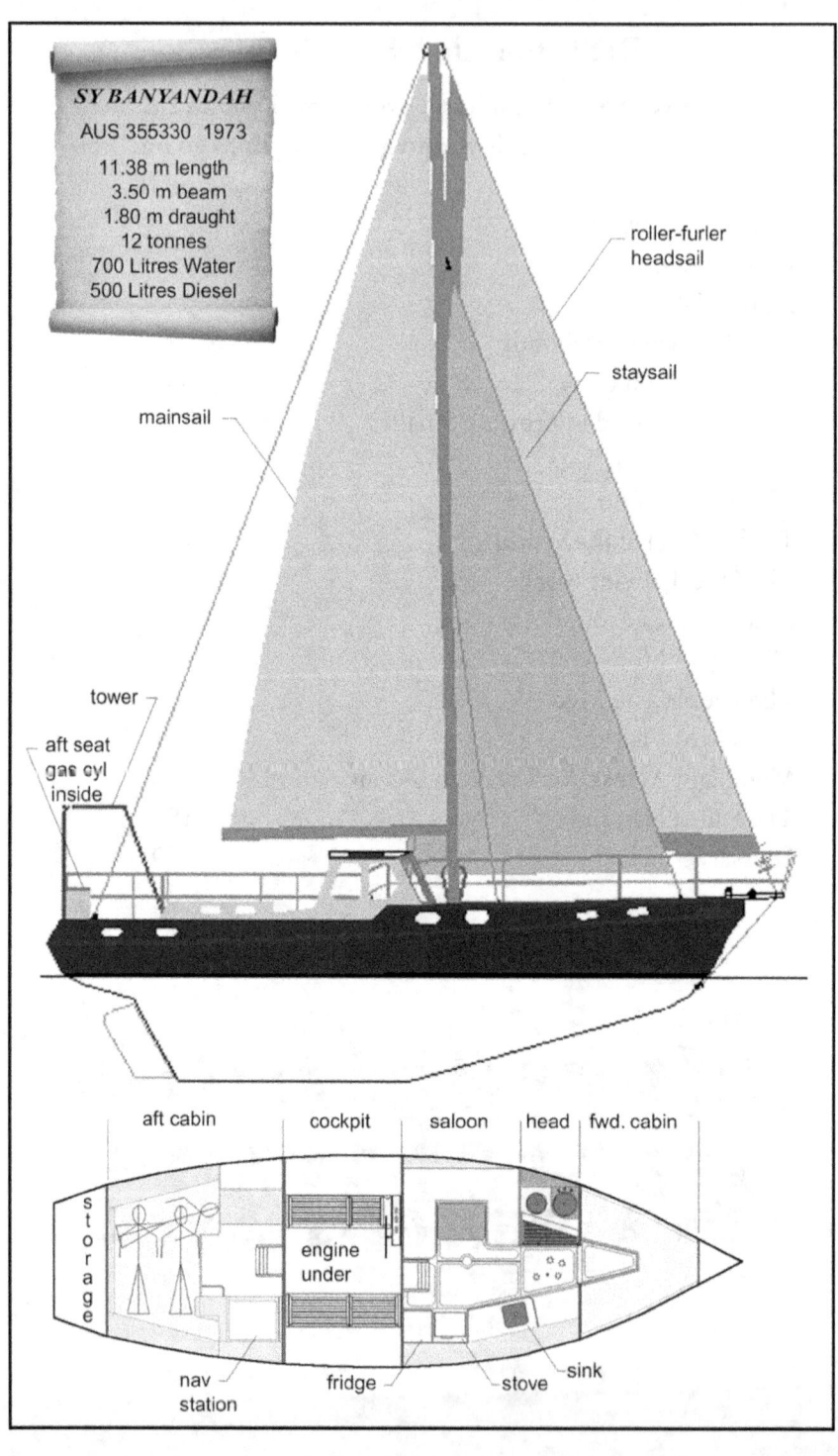

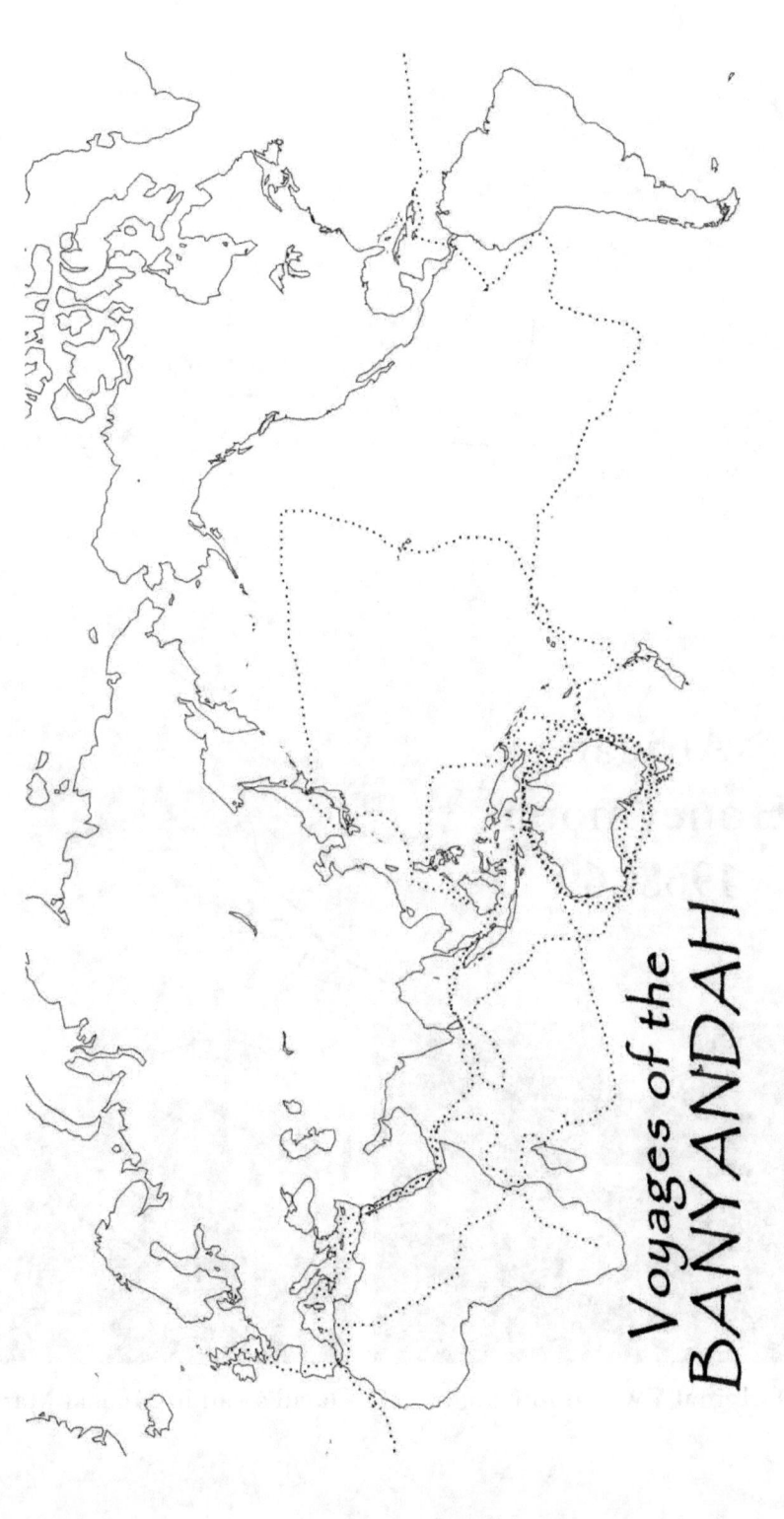

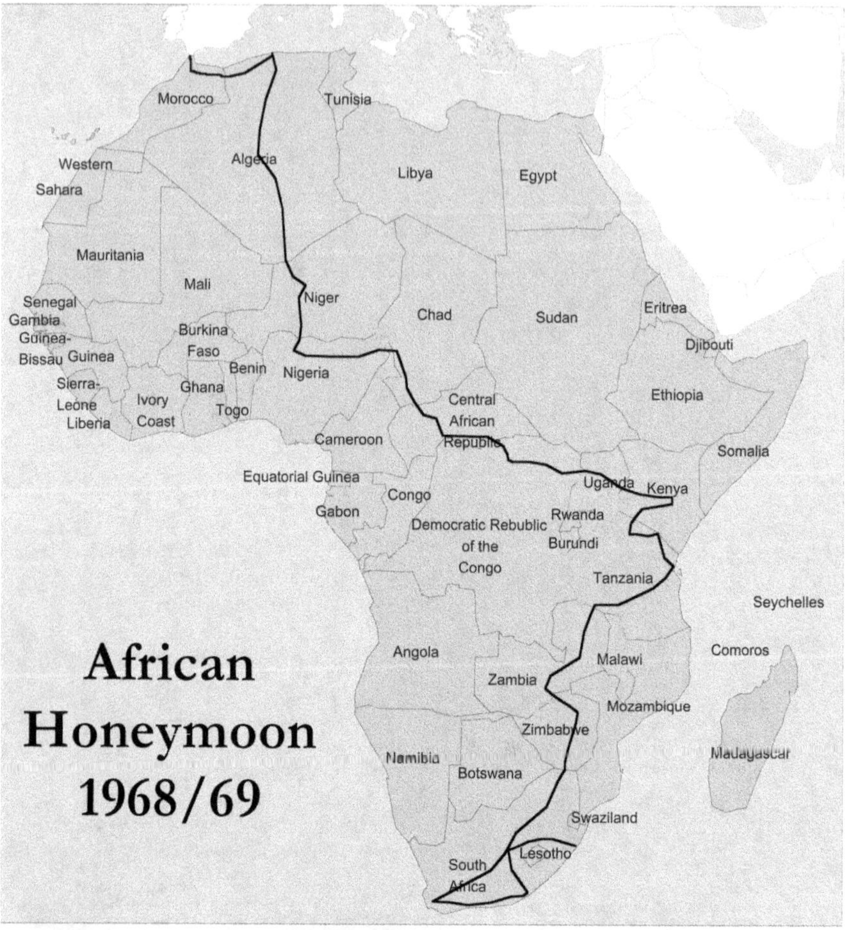

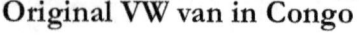

African Honeymoon 1968/69

Original VW van in Congo

David's van in Maasai Mara

AFRICAN HONEYMOON
For my Judith, my anchor, compass, and shipmate.
WE MUST HAVE BEEN CRAZY

When we were just kids and about to be married, we bought a rusty VW van that had languished in a field for nearly forever. Our first sight of it was a pair of sad eyes, its divided windscreen peeking over tall grass, so we bought that cute little box. Not out of pity, but thinking we could use its new tyres on our honeymoon trip to Southern Africa.

Only crazies buy the wheels and tyres first

Almost new, we could use those mud and snow tyres and the rest could be spares, so we paid the farmer his asking price of 25 quid.

A set of wheels! Hooray! Hooray! We were on our way to Africa. Our joy knew no bounds for a few minutes, at least until my lovely bride wanted to know, "How to get it home?"

The farmer didn't want just the wheels taken away; he wanted the whole mess out of sight.

But it couldn't be driven away. Not only was it not registered, the engine didn't work.

In the next few months our wedding plans proceeded to schedule, which is a lot more than can be said for finding a better van to fit those lovely mud and snow tyres. And that left us in a pickle with no other choice but to restore 'old sad eyes.' So that ol' bucket of rust was dragged over hill and dale to a new home in my future mother-in-law's driveway. Once parked there we played house within its hollow shell, imagining life together. To rid the feeling of living in a box, from the wreckers we got some side windows that brightened her up. Then in the days that followed, as a team we de-rusted and bogged her shell, installed our matrimonial bed, a sink and a stove, and a few cupboards. To have a reliable vehicle, we decided that the engine must be pulled apart and rebuilt with whatever it needed. The engine didn't take much to get her started and then installing new brakes made 'old sad eyes' a runner even if her underside wasn't too pretty. Then another buying spree at our helpful wrecker saw us replace the hard bench seat with two luxurious Jaguar red leather seats. They not only added a touch of class, they also provided far more comfort. The big day came at last. No, not for our wedding, but rather a roadworthy examination from mum Grey's mechanic. He would pass it – but only if we promised to drive it straight out the country!

Off for Africa - Southampton to Ceuta by ferry - 25 November 1968

To everyone's surprise, we got out of England even though my new bride had to push start our baby or we'd never have boarded the Southampton ferry on time. My oh my, that rather inauspicious start saw several minor problems become big trouble, like when chugging towards the summit of the Atlas Mountains separating North Africa from the huge expanse of the Sahara Desert.

Fired up with expectations of a happy life together, our honeymoon smiles quickly vanished when our van lurched, followed by screeching metal. Next came a strange vision, our rear wheel rolling past the driver's window before catapulting over the cliff face.

Fortunately we didn't follow it to our deaths. Instead, I was soon dragging the offending wheel back up the ravine and reattaching it using nuts snaffled from the other wheel hubs. When again a going concern, happiness returned, until we discovered the offending tyre had ripped a hole through the rear engine compartment. Oh well. Not a bother. Stuffing some old newspaper into it got us on the road again. But like a rock thrown into deep water, its ripples were to go on and on.

A photo taken of us celebrating our first month of marital bliss shows us embracing at the edge of the Tademait Plateau. Behind us the tarmac had ended, and the view ahead was nothing but sand and black rock to the distant horizon. Before us lay two thousand kilometres of wilderness with very little water.

As we traversed down the rocky escarpment, the wilderness seemed strangely beautiful which caused our excitement to grow. We were together as husband and wife and about to face one of Earth's greatest challenges. How sweet it all seemed. Then the ridge ran down to a flat plateau very much like the world's largest parking lot made by an unending expanse of small black pebbles. Getting out, beneath the pebbles lay only sand.

Coasting along, our tensions were beginning to ease when the VW's horizontal four cylinder engine started sounding a bit ragged. But not for long. Soon the engine just quit. Taking a look at the back, our worst fears were dispelled when sighting the engine still on its mounts.

But why had it stopped? We had fuel. We had crank.

And why was the air filter so heavy? Opening it up we discovered there was simply no space left for air. It was choked solid with sand stained black by whatever oil had been there to trap nasty sharp things like that Saharan sand.

Clearing the filter and refilling it with fresh oil got us going across the black plains again, but that unfortunate incident marked the start of the VW's demise.

Next morning, even though the engine rapidly cranked, she refused to start. Engine compression had gone and push starting began. So from that moment on, we only parked on level ground, or better still, facing downhill.

Arrived Tamanrasset - 28 December 68 – 2740 km in Africa

Upon arriving at the last Algerian outpost of Tamanrasset, Christmas didn't matter to the Muslim nomads, but New Year did as it brought a week's holiday with it. Therefore we had a decision to make – either cool our heels for another week while the border was closed or leave before nightfall.

Of course being young and in love we couldn't wait. So we filled every container with fuel then chugged past the lift gate to begin the longest stretch of desert just as the sun slipped below the sandy horizon. So impetuous were we, a kettle and an old inner tube contained our total drinking water, which had to last us until the next well, nine hundred kilometres south in Niger.

To be alone and completely surrounded by nature can be a warm wonderful feeling, as long as you are safe. But we didn't feel safe. In fact we felt quite frightened by dark thoughts of getting bogged in Sahara sand with no other traffic coming along for a week.

During our second day, we met a tribe of nomadic Tuareg, the men appearing so proud and fearless riding atop their camels in flowing jellabas with swirls of cloth protecting their heads. Meeting them in such a lonely place at first heightened our fear, but we were 'saved' when a small boy giggled from behind his mother's robes then leapt to the front to get a closer look at the strangers.

Laughing with him we ruffled his hair and that broke the ice.

What a relief to be warmly greeted while coarse rugs were spread upon the sand so that refreshments could be served. One moment fearful, the next we were enjoying an unusual encounter. Soon we were choking down sweet camel's milk still steaming from the chipped porcelain bowl used to collect it while marvelling at our good fortune.

An old man, whose skin resembled the dates we were tasting, caught our eye with a raised eyebrow then a crooked finger indicating he wanted some water to drink. Handing him our kettle, we became fixated as the gleam in his eyes grew just before he poured every drop into his leather water bag.

What could we do, it was gone.

Driving off in the low afternoon sun, a few kilometres further on we started to bog and I dodged left then right searching for firmer ground, all the while sinking slowly deeper until the VW sat silently on its frame. But we didn't despair. After all we were young and in love and still had half an inner tube of water and slept that night snuggled up together under a full moon adding brightness to the clear heavens full of stars.

First light next day we managed to escape by cutting sand mat strips from the plywood base that supported the gear on our roof-rack. Along them we pushed our VW onto firmer sand. We were now deep within the Sahara with no trees in sight, nothing in fact but an unending vista of yellow sand, and we got along fine for most of the day, that is until we encountered a mishmash of intersecting tracks. Stopping the van on what seemed firm flat sand, we unloaded the little motorbike carried across the back then took off to explore the way ahead. We found many tracks leading off to deep holes made by others digging themselves out, but then luckily found one that went to a 44 gallon drum marking better surface.

Some time later after negotiating all that, in fact when a short day's run before the first outpost in Niger, there came an almighty bang followed by a deafening silence after the engine blew up.

African Honeymoon

When the cold night air was being heated up by a naked sun, filthy from our waterless travels I slid under the VW to examine the engine. And as I lay there scratching my head, I'm astonished by a young man riding out the heat haze on a bicycle. Without hesitation he stops and says in French that he's going to town and offered to come back with some water. Watching him disappear back into the heat haze started me wondering if I'd been dreaming, and even more determined I went back to finding the problem.

What I discovered was that the gizmos operating the valves had pulled out. What a dilemma. Desert nights are cold, desert days are hot, so we did pretty much nothing except chase shade around the sides of the van that day. My night's sleep brought the answer. I always come up with the best ideas in bed and minutes after getting up I had fixed the problem by driving a bolt through the fins to refasten the rockers. Push-starting the van, the engine fired first piston up - just as the boy showed up with several cans of water and saying the local mechanic would soon be coming.

Who needed him I thought and away we went, rumbling down the track only to be confronted by a *"deux chevaux"* popping above a crest, scooting over the sand like an intoxicated Thorny Devil.

Well, it whizzed past, a big thumbs up and congratulating smile on the dark man's face. Suddenly he spun her around and shot past us with a huge farewell wave and then disappeared back over the crest without even slowing down. Instantly alone again, our exuberance evaporated leaving us fearing another mishap increasing in the rising heat.

We got into Agadez late that day, but the front suspension wasn't happy with our beaut new tyres squealing on the underside of the wheel wells. Luck must follow the young and bold because in the middle of nowhere we had passed a burnt-out VW and had snaffled its front suspension, lashing it atop our roof racks.

Agadez was just a lonely outpost consisting of three small sandy streets surrounded by miles and miles of more sand. Near the minaret we found the Thorny Devil and then the local French mechanic who made us very welcome by allowing us to park in his drive, where I immediately started changing over the suspension.

Quite soon after dark a big scene erupted. Across the back of the van our 70cc motorbike had aroused much attention as we drove into town with a number of kids chasing after us. Unfortunately the Police Chief fancied it. Even more dangerous, so did the Immigration Chief. Suddenly right in front of our eyes a bidding war began in a language we couldn't understand. We didn't want to sell the bike but it soon became obvious that if we didn't, we'd have bigger troubles. When the bartering stopped, the immigration man gruffly handed me a gigantic pile of Central African Francs indicating it was either take it or go back.

A day or two later a convoy of vehicles arrived, the first after the holidays. At its head was a Greek man who had purchased a number of un-roadworthy Mercedes Benz in Germany that he was shifting to sell in Nigeria. The line of vehicles was complete with a tow truck and bus. Tagging along to help shift the sand mats were a half dozen European hitchhikers including three English who had had their van confiscated in Tamanrasset.

How quickly things change. With our big pile of Central African cash, we opened a bank and started changing their dollars and pounds so they could buy food and fuel. Then early the next morning we set off for Zinder, thinking it'd be better to be in front of such a well equipped convoy in case we got stuck again.

The first day out the terrain turned soft again and while grinding through it with the engine screaming we heard an explosion then hissing and snorting every cycle before abruptly stopping with what had sounded like a hole in a piston.

This could be far more dangerous than before because there were several tracks leading to Zinder. In the eerie silence that enveloped us, worried that the convoy would pass by a different track, all we could do was wait for what seemed hours peering in every direction across the shimmering desert. Then a dust cloud appeared on the horizon. Figuring it would pass about a kilometre away, we raced across the soft sand, desperate to flag down the Greek.

Discussions followed. What to do? Leave the van to procure spares or tow it. Fearing human vultures, a tow was arranged and although it saved our possessions, it nearly cost us our lives.

Washboard roads feature in the southern Sahara and we soon discovered that each vehicle needed a different speed to float atop the ridges. And because the tow truck had to travel at a speed faster than us, the VW got hopelessly out of sync. We'd hit the crests, fly into the air, and then fall back into the ruts, all the time being hauled along attached by a steel chain. Bouncing along engulfed in his dust, it soon became a nightmare intently watching for his looming dark shape which told me when to hit the brakes.

But our situation was far worse than that. Even before reaching Tamanrasset we had lost the passenger side window in a bizarre encounter with the only vehicle seen in days, and now the dust being thrown up was pouring in, blinding my dear lovely wife. The tow truck couldn't see us either. Choking on dust, it took forever for him to respond to her frantically waving her straw-hat out the window. And when he finally pulled over, my wife a mess with thick orange desert makeup and matted hair, he could only offer her a pair of motorcycle glasses. It was that or unhitch the van.

Getting going again, the bumper was gone; crushed under us somewhere en-route. And the headlights had fallen out. And all the bog so lovingly shaped, it gone too. Soon the phenomena of the bumps vibrated all the brake fluid out the reservoir, creating the horrific situation of only being able to stop by using the handbrake. That discovery very nearly killed us when we almost hit the back of the truck. Fortunately when it became dark, it actually became easier because whenever the slack chain hit the rocky track, sparks flew up making it easier to judge when to pull the handbrake.

Arrived Zinder, Jude in tears - 19 January 1969 – 3,860 km inside Africa

More trouble. The mechanic in Agadez had written a note to a mechanic in Zinder, both were Frenchmen, and while staying at his workshop we discovered the VW's chassis had cracked!

Three days later we took a bus trip to Kano in Nigeria for the required engine parts, but visa problems at the border stopped me from entering. I could have gone in but my Nigerian visa was good for only one entry, which we'd need later. The only place to get a new one was on the other side of the desert at Niamey, 1000 kilometres away. So while Jude went on alone into war torn Nigeria, I spent the night at the Kongolum border crossing talking about life and the Biafran War with the head immigration official visiting from Kano.

In a sense, it can be said that the British were the cause of the Biafran Civil War, which was at its height when we were there in early 1969.

When the African continent was colonized by Britain and other European nations, they split it up based on their own interests. They didn't try to figure out which areas really belonged together and conveniently neglected religious, linguistic, and ethnic differences. What they created were new political entities that had never existed before.

More than fifty years earlier, Great Britain had formed what would become Nigeria from an area of West Africa containing hundreds of different ethnic groups. There were three predominant ones: the Igbo, which formed about 70% of the population in the southeast; the Hausa-Fulani, forming about 65% of the peoples in the northern part of the territory; and the Yoruba, about 75% of the population in the southwest. Many differences occurred between these groups. For example, the Hausa were Muslim and had a system of government that was relatively feudal. In contrast, the Igbo were mainly Christian and had a more democratic society. The first Governor General of Nigeria, Sir Hugh Clifford stated that while Southern Province Nigerians were educated to the extent that skilled labour was readily available and many had become professionals like doctors and lawyers; no Northern Province Nigerians were "sufficiently educated to enable them to fill the most minor clerical posts in the office of any government department." Nevertheless, the British lumped them all together when creating Nigeria.

After 1960 when Nigeria became independent, this led to conflicts between the Hausa and the Igbo as to who should have power in the new country. The conflicts between them eventually led the Igbo to secede and form a new country that they called Biafra. The 'Biafran War' was fought to prevent the secession and to force that region back into the country of Nigeria.

At the border crossing I learnt that the Federal side expected a quick victory. But we now know the Biafrans fought the war as a means of survival and were ready to fight to the last man.

Making it somewhat better and far worse for us, within this volatile atmosphere was another power struggle between the military and police.

The next day Jude returned from Kano pretty hyped up, telling stories of arrest and danger in war torn Nigeria and of a night spent in jail.

Back in Zinder, I rebuilt the engine with the new parts and welded the frame with a gas torch but while doing this, inadvertently burst the front brake line with the flame, losing the driver's side front brake.

We reached Kano in Nigeria on the 28th of January and drove directly to the police station for a safe place to stay, where we discovered that the frame had cracked for the second time. Fortunately just down the dusty street we had a thin plate welded over it by a roadside repairman using an ancient acetylene pellet gas welder. On our first afternoon wandering about the immensely crowded streets we bumped into the three white faces of the Englishmen who had had their van confiscated in Tamanrasset. In Kano they'd just bought a well used VW van to continue their travels. Theirs is an intriguing tale. Four had set out from England together but one got jack of the hardship and bolted at Tamanrasset, accidently taking the car's rego papers in his kit. This hadn't been a problem until the other three had tried to exit Algeria. Unable to produce the required document, the border guards confiscated their van, and towed it to the police compound. This infuriated the lads so much they snuck in late that night and poured sand into the fuel tank. Unfortunately they got caught, and were charged with destroying government property. We'd heard this story from the British High Commissioner in Algiers when I was applying for my Nigerian visa. The High Commissioner adamantly told us to stay out the region, warning us that they were washing their hands of such troubles.

When the three English lads needed more time to fix up their van, I magnanimously suggested they should see my new mate, the immigration chief I met at the border. Feeling perky like a strutting peacock I lead the lads in, but instead of the expected cordial greeting an indignant tongue lashed us for daring to be so audacious. Aghast, our passports were promptly confiscated and all of us were ordered to leave the country, back the way we'd come. Under guard they escorted us to the Police Station, and there, proving there is a saviour, when the coast was clear the friendly Police Chief said, "Here are your papers. Best you get out of Kano." Wink, wink.

Two vans together, instead of going back the way we'd come, we drove east to the Catholic mission at Maiduguri where Jude and I stayed just the one night, leaving the three English behind fixing their van.

Across the flat floodplain of Cameroon we drove, arriving at Fort Foureau in one day. Then we crossed the Chari River to enter Chad at Fort Lami. Now we were 5,000 kilometres into Africa.

French influence was obvious and there were many more Europeans. The market's open spaces, full of dried fish and roughly butchered meat sold by the handful, were dominated by a clay arched hall bustling with colourfully costumed ladies selling small piles of veggies, mostly beans and chillies and weird shaped gourds. We obtained visas for the Congo then left on February 11th for Bongor then Doba.

Arrived Bangui, Central African Republic - 17 February 1969
5.960 km since Tangiers

The engine was still in bad shape as we progressed down the great continent, our problems condensing into three types; physical, political and an emotional roller-coaster. The gaping hole in the engine compartment, made when the tyre flew off, eventually forced us to rebuild the engine on three separate occasions.

Imagine us newlyweds in a capital city, filthy like street urchins, wandering into a mechanic's garage and asking where we could get VW engine parts. Then without speaking a word, the French mechanic looked us up and down before wandering outside to look at our van. Inside his garage, bits of engines filled every greasy bench top. When he returned shaking his head, we were certain he would do nothing for us. Then a wry smile spread across his grease smeared face as he nodded towards the floor saying in French, "Will those do?" There in a row stood four VW pots with pistons and rings. Completely stunned we of course beamed back our thanks. Language wasn't a problem. Hardly a word was spoken. He simply winked, gave us the thumbs up then pointed us out his shop.

Bangui, the capital of the C.A.R. had many impressive buildings next to a large central park that ran along the banks of the Ubangui River. While driving along its tree lined road and seeing open grass in the park, we shrugged our shoulders and headed straight onto it.

This was our third time removing the engine on the fly, so we were experts. The motorbike, long gone, and no rear bumper meant we only had to remove four bolts to drop the engine onto the spare tire where we changed the cylinders and pistons, and had it running again in less than three hours.

Fast as we were a huge crowd of locals soon gathered, all gesticulating and jabbering in various tongues. Don't think they'd ever seen a white lady with grease across her face swing a spanner before.

All was going swimmingly when through the black crowd pushed a white face making me gasp, thinking we were in deep trouble. Oddly, the weed thin man introduced himself in proper English as David, the local school teacher, and asked would we like to stay at his place.

We said we'd like to but declined, telling him we planned to be gone later that day. We were in a hurry to reach East Africa and leave behind all the political unrest.

You can imagine our excitement as we approached the ferry landing, ready to cross the Ubangui River. Well! We were utterly disappointed when we saw the sign declaring it Closed! It seemed there was a feud between President Bokassa and General Mobutu over streetlights erected in the tiny town on the other side of the river in the Congo. There were none in Bangui, the capital of the C.A.R.

While at the ferry a large green Bedford delivery van drove up. It had a spare wheel on the roof next to a replacement radiator, and a tall lanky Pom jumped out sporting a patchy beard and introduced himself as another David. Inside were Charles, wimpish thin with ginger hair, and short, feisty Stewart. The three lads were also looking for a way to cross the river. So I explained what had happened and told them that I was going to get the embassies to help.

Jude and I stayed at the teacher's house after all and David really enjoyed our enlightened discourse. It proved a good place while attempting to gain the help of the embassies. Over the next few days we pursued the Dutch, French, and Danish consulates, plus we had an audience with the country's Number 2, Bokassa's cousin. But no help came from anyone. That was a let-down that increased our worry about being able to complete our journey. Especially as we were running short of money and had to transit the Congo to reach East Africa because civil war raged in the Sudan. Our anxiety became even worse when we discovered that the steel patch over our broken chassis had split apart. It was uncanny because the steering wheel moved closer to the driver and the engine raced when the throttle cable effectively became shorter the more the van collapsed.

Before starting more days bumping along country tracks we had to re-weld the chassis under the driver seat. The crack was near where the front wheel attached. We approached a different mechanic. He must have thought I looked the part, being so filthy, and in a do it yourself manner handed me a bunch of electrodes and a helmet. The problem was I had never electric welded before. But through all the confusion and language problems I thought, well, it couldn't be that hard, so I removed the wheel and attempted to weld up the crack. But the helmet was so dark, so useless I threw it down and just squinted while splotching puddles of metal until my eyes began to water. Driving away with blisters under my eyelids, Jude had to drive. It was really fortunate we were staying with the English teacher. He gave me his bed and I lay flat on my back, pretty much blind under a massive mosquito net while outside for three days torrential rain fell. I can't describe how thankful I felt when my sight returned.

Politically the border still remained closed when the van with the other English lads showed up. It hadn't gone easy for them either and when they heard the bad news that the ferry was closed, they sold their van and took the steamer to Kinshasa. Jude and I had other ideas. We'd build a raft out of the many fuel drums found around the town and use them to float ourselves across the river. Crazy, yeah – but hey, we were young and in love and pretty much invincible.

It took a few days to line up enough drums to construct the raft then two things happened. The police hauled us in to caution us against disobeying the President, and while at the police station lanky tall David showed up. Walking outside with him, after telling him our tale of woe, he blurted out that they were going to drive to the Sudan where they hoped to go cross-country to Uganda. Taking him back to the teacher's house, we held a war council, where, aided by the teacher's road map we elected to travel together and look for a ferry still crossing the river in every town en-route to the Sudan.

Three bumpy, dirty days later, as we came over a rise our hearts stopped beating. The muddy Ubangui was cutting a swath through green jungle and upon it down below a motorized punt was bringing a small car across from the Congo.

Had they not heard of Bokassa's decree?

The history of the Republic of the Congo is even more bizarre than Nigeria's. Colonial rule began in the late 19th century when King Leopold II of Belgium attempted to persuade the Belgian government to support colonial expansion around the then-largely unexplored Congo Basin. The Belgian government's ambivalence led the King to create the colony on his own, with support from a number of Western countries who viewed Leopold as a useful buffer between rival colonial powers. By the turn of the century, the violence of Free State officials against indigenous Congolese, along with their ruthless economic extraction, led Belgium to take control, which officially it did in 1908, creating the Belgian Congo.

That's part one of a tragic story of greed and lust for power that was further ignited by world events. The Congo's rich natural resources, including uranium - much of the uranium used by the U.S. nuclear programme during World War II was Congolese - led to substantial interest in the region from both the Soviet Union and the United States, especially as the Cold War developed.

During the 1950s, an African nationalist movement developed in the Belgian Congo, primarily among the "évolués," the new middle class of Europeanised Africans in the cities. A long history of fractional dissent lead various black groups from different regions to call for independence. There were many riots, leading the white community to become increasingly radicalised. As law and order began to break down, white civilians formed militia groups to police their neighbourhoods. These militias frequently attacked the blacks. In the fallout from the Léopoldville riots, in January 1960, the Belgium government launched a high-profile conference in Brussels. They had hoped for a period of at least 30 years before independence, but Congolese pressure led to 30 June 1960 being set as the date. Of course with so many factions at work in a resource rich, education poor area similar in size to Western Australia but clad in thick jungle, there were countless uprising and killings of both blacks and whites. One of these rebel groups called themselves "Simba" (Kiswahili for "lion"), and they had a vague ideology loosely based on communism that prioritised equality and aimed to increase overall wealth. These rebels founded a state, the People's Republic of the Congo with its capital at Stanleyville. This new state was supported by the Soviet Union and China, which supplied it with arms. It was also supported by Cuba, which sent a team of over 100 advisors led by Che Guevara. The Simba rebellion coincided with a wide escalation of the Cold War and it's been speculated that had the rebellion not been rapidly defeated, a full-scale American military intervention could have occurred as in Vietnam.

During the Congo Crisis in 1960, Belgian forces aided Colonel Mobutu in a coup against the nationalist government of Patrice Lumumba, who was the first democratically elected leader. Lumumba was subsequently executed by a Katangese firing squad led by Julien Gat, a Belgian mercenary. Mobutu then assumed the role of army chief of staff, before taking power directly in a second coup in 1965. As part of his program of "national authenticity," Mobutu changed the Congo's name to Zaïre in 1971 and his own name to Mobutu Sese Seko in 1972. Supported in office primarily by Belgium and the United States, he formed an authoritarian regime, amassed vast personal wealth, and attempted to purge the country of all colonial cultural influence while enjoying considerable support due to his anti-communist stance.

When we were there in 1969 there were many elements of the much feared Simba still prowling around the northeast corner of the Congo, which we had to transit.

As we got nearer to central Africa we heard many stories of atrocities in the Congo, but we just thought them exaggerated until that ferry landed and an elderly lady literally fell to the ground sobbing hysterically. On her knees, she passionately kissed the black soil of the Central African Republic. Later she told us about the Stanleyville massacre, one of the most savage crimes of the last century, the cold-blooded massacre of hostages by the Simba rebels.

There were nearly three hundred white hostages imprisoned in the Victoria Hotel when the sun rose over Stanleyville on 24 November 1964. A few hours later, seconds before their rescuers arrived, many lay dead, brutally hacked to death or shot by their rebel captors. Others, the lucky ones, would thank God that they had survived the premeditated and cold-blooded slaughter.

By November a year later, mercenaries led by Lt Colonel Mike Hoare had effectively suppressed the Lion rebellion. However, holdouts of the rebels continued their insurgency until the 1990s.

Jude was the only lady with us and we all turned to her. She merely shrugged because as she's explained since, her father had been her strength, having told her once, "take chances and you'll achieve great things." With Jude's non-plus reaction, the rest of us after very few words decided, "Oh, what the hell." So we made arrangements to cross the next day, the 12th of March.

Next morning we discovered that the ferry was a relic from WW II, that it leaked like a sieve through holes along its bottom that were plugged with wads of paper, and that two boys bailed continuously, one in each hull. So when the captain said we would cross one at a time, we feared being split up, and insisted on going together. But before loading the vans he took David and I across to negotiate with the military. Of course they wanted money or booze to let us in, but having neither, eventually agreed to let us in if we transported some of the soldiers back to their base.

Loading the vans over rickety ramps scared the living daylights out of me thinking we'd be in dire straits should they collapse or the ferry sink. Thank God neither happened.

Landing in the Congo, for Jude's safety we agreed that only David would transport the soldiers. Naturally all of them carried automatic weapons. Once they had piled into his large delivery van he drove off into the jungle with us close behind. But when the exuberant soldiers began firing their automatic rifles out the double rear doors, we immediately dropped back to avoid any stray bullets that might come our way. Scary hey?

We stayed at the Catholic mission at Monga, straight away hearing stories of torture and rape, followed by a warning, "Do not stop for any reason!"

That sounded like good advice, especially as we still had a thousand kilometres to transit before our seven day visas expired and be turned back. Or worse still, arrested. Basically the roads were narrow muddy tracks through dense jungle, dotted with pools and deep divots created when heavy trucks became bogged. Along the edge of this wilderness, bamboo forests flourished as if towering rocket launchers. From these, markers had been cut and placed so vehicles wouldn't fall into the quagmire, and guided the few brave enough to cross the sapling corduroy. These were tricky for us, our van slipping and sliding as the platforms unbalanced with its weight. After nearly coming to grief on the first few, we learned to put on full power to get across as quickly as we could. Bridge crossings over streams and gullies were even more dangerous. They were crossed atop tree trunks laid together, and sometimes a log had collapsed leaving a gap, forcing us to choose carefully which logs to put our wheels on.

The V.W.'s front suspension collapsing yet again forced us to cut holes into the cabin to allow the tyres to come up, meaning mud was also slung inside, splattering us and our windscreen. The wet sludge shorting out the windscreen wipers.

Day number two we crossed the Uele River by a pole driven punt, a strenuous effort fighting current, then replenished our fuel at the cotton gin in Buta where there was no food except a few tins of fish. Although having few provisions, we dared not stop at villages. But, after passing one, when a dozen scrawny chickens ran from thick vegetation and scurried directly in front of our van, basic instinct took control. I pushed the pedal to the metal, hot in pursuit, hitting one bird square on the van's V.W. round insignia. Catapulted high into the air, the hapless creature hit a tree, and I slammed on the brakes to stop near where the dead bird fell, and Jude jumped out and ran back to get it. As she grabbed the bird, angry villagers streamed out the jungle, and she ran for her life, while I revved up our old battered machine to flee from the mob.

About every hundred kilometres were roadblocks manned by soliders brandishing machineguns. After stopping at one and being sent back to get a signature from the last checkpoint, we held our nerve and ran through the rest of them with Judith face down on the floor.

About halfway we stayed at the mission at Poko, where the fathers looked more like escaped Nazi's in white gowns and long beards down to very fat bellies. And yet they were very helpful, providing plenty of good food, especially, delicious huge blocks of cheese and fresh fruit.

Running in such arduous conditions was very hard on poor old sad eyes. When we heard noises coming from a rear wheel, I removed the brake drum and found that the hydraulic cylinder had been ripped loose. Its remains had been tumbling into bits. Yet another hydraulic line was pinched closed leaving only one brake remaining. Not all of our journey through the Congo was hair-raising though. At times it was a huge relief just to stop on the road and breathe in the rainforest air. Other times we were stopped by natural obstacles like a swarm of brightly coloured butterflies drinking from the muddy road, or army ants in two lines forming a corridor protecting workers carrying eggs, moving their nest site across the road.

Driving through the town of Isiro, ornate colonial buildings stood abandoned and overgrown. Called Paulis before independence, it was the capital of Haut-Uele District in the northeast. Through the door-less entries we saw natives around cooking fires and wondered if they were burning the doors and furniture. Just four years earlier, The Reverend Joseph Tucker, a 49-year-old veteran Assemblies of God missionary to the Congo, was brutally beaten to death by Congolese rebels. According to the United Press International, the beating of the Rev. Tucker took 45 minutes - "one stroke at a time with each stroke coming after his groaning from the previous stroke ended."

The Rev. Tucker was reported to have been among an estimated 60 Europeans and Americans herded into the Dominican Mission at Paulis, where these beatings were administered. Reports indicate that the bodies of 20 of the 60 were thrown into a nearby crocodile-infested river.

As we bumped our way into Watsa, which lies just a couple kilometres from the Ugandan border, the engine began to roar and the steering wheel inched closer, nearly touching my tummy. It would seem good fortune favours fools as well as the young in love because we found a small gold mine and a proper thick plate was welded over our cracked frame. Unfortunately they could not straighten the van's swayed back. Knowing how dangerous the van had become, Jude transferred into David's van for the last bit of rough track before the border.

David had his own problems. His van hadn't a *carnet de passage*, that's the bond lodged in the home country guaranteeing export from the countries travelled through if you got stuck. In the condition our van was in, we surely didn't want ours recorded, we'd lose our bond if we ditched our van, so he and I decided we'd try and bluff our way into East Africa.

Arua, Uganda – 7,400 km in Africa

If we got into East Africa we'd have half a chance of reaching South Africa and find paid employment which we desperately wanted. But with no bumper, the headlights taped in place, the doors wired shut and a swayed back, our chances of being granted entry seemed rather slim. Therefore when the border hut came into view we left the vans parked a long way up the road and waltzed in with our papers ready. David and I kept up a jovial banter, continuously asking questions, hoping the two black African officials would let us through. And by their comments they would, if we produced our *carnet de passage*. Every time it came up we waved our British rego papers which were heavy buff coloured cards folded in three with each year's payment stamped and initialled on the last page. The poor officials jabbering back and forth were a bit confounded. Worried we'd be refused, David and I kept smiling and nodding and pointing to our car documents. After much ado they came to some agreement between themselves. Those poor officials would have had difficulty reading the English and deciding which bit to retain. But in the end one heavily stamped a leaf in each of the folded rego's then tore off the last part and stuck them in their files.

Like a marathon runner breaking the finish tape there was great elation as we cleared that last major hurdle. David went through the raised gate first, and behind him I didn't hesitate or slow down, bolting through with my foot hard on the pedal. As if coming out of a bad dream, almost immediately the foothills smoothed into a lush green river valley. On a much improved road David kept the pace up until we spied a wide river coming up. At a rather temporary looking bridge, he pulled over next to a sign declaring this to be the White Nile. Leaving the three lads posing for photos, I slipped up behind my love and embraced her. Feeling her warmth, she smelt sweet with animal sweat, but under it, her energy filled me with love and so I whispered in her ear, "Come with me, the road ahead is much safer. Let's lose the lads for awhile."

I could never imagine travelling to such magnificent places and not being able to share them with the love of my life. "One day," I whispered, "I'll take you to the end of this river and together we'll touch the tombs of the once mighty pharaohs."

Jude swung around in my grip, and the kiss we shared erased all the pain and fear we had endured since embarking upon our African honeymoon. Somehow, I can't explain it, but at that moment we merged together and became one.

Across that bridge magic happened when alone on that lonely road entering the Murchison Falls National Park. Right before us a herd of elephants crossed our path. Our first wild animals, fantastic!! We had not imagined seeing such huge wild creatures right in front of us. Several enormous bulls were flapping huge ears, leading more dainty cows shepherding cute little baby calves. And they weren't in a zoo. These animals were in control of their own destinies with a big fellow as guard. Flat open grasses filled the other side of the road, and where the herd went we saw the funniest critters. With tails erect, puff balls at the tips like feather dusters, black wart hogs were racing erratically in all directions, with their dusters last seen disappearing into the tall grass.

Hardly another mile further on, the road was filled with gazelles. They were such graceful creatures we were mesmerized snapping photos of their swirling horns and beautiful colours.

The ride to Kampala on the new bitumen road was a prize worth all our efforts, but the sound of more metal tearing accompanied us on that smooth ride, reminding us how dangerous our van had become.

Kampala, Uganda - 20 March 69 – 8,210 km in Africa

The road to Kampala passed through agricultural land, very neat and organised for the first time since North Africa.

Pulling into Kampala's city park, over dinner with the three lads we let them know we could not continue in our van. It was far too unsafe, but now that we were in a safer part of Africa, we were going to hitchhike the rest of the way to South Africa.

The Bedford was David's van. The other two only contributed to its running costs, and he in his clipped speech asked, "Why not join us? We could use some extra funds."

After all we'd been through together, his offer brought Jude to tears and she rapturously hugged him while the others and I monkeyed around shouting, "We're off to Cape Town, we are, we are."

Going with David to South Africa gave us the opportunity of providing a house for one of the local impoverished families living in cardboard boxes. And needing money to pay David, we sold our van which still had a stove and bed. Not for much. We basically passed it on for the same bargain price we'd given the farmer. But, knowing Africa, we suspect that it became a taxi within a week.

It was sad unloading our personal stuff. Every trinket brought back memories. I even caressed the table I'd made, and the bed. But when we handed it over to the Bantu family of six and saw the uplifting gleam of happiness, we were emotionally charged with hope that everyone would benefit.

Travelling in David's van forced an immediate adjustment. Not only did we not have our own space, I was no longer in charge. But that was countered by being a part of a larger team which brought forth even bigger, more challenging ideas. David casually suggested that we divert and climb Mt. Kenya, something Jude and I would not have attempted on our own. But it really appealed to us and with three additional lads we formed a strong team. And we had camping gear and just about enough warm clothes, so we agreed to make an assault on Africa's second highest peak at 5,199 m.

Entered Kenya at Malaba – 24 March 69

Leaving Kampala early the next morning we followed the road around Lake Victoria and in a few easy hours arrived at Malaba, the border with Kenya. The East African countries of Uganda, Kenya, and Tanzania had once been British colonies, therefore crossing between them was easy, and the question of a *carnet de passage* never arose again. Light drizzle fell as we passed though Eldoret, the countryside changing so little that we hardly noticed an inconspicuous sign marking the Equator. In fact David had to back track so we could get a photo of our first time crossing into the Southern Hemisphere. Later in the day we came into the small town of Nakuru, with the recently declared Nakuru National Park nearby where we intended camping that night. Gathering supplies at the tiny store we drove the last few kilometres down a dirt track, past a crude park sign then following another that pointed off track we came to a small stone shack with the single word "Warden." A pitifully dressed black fellow called Tommy greeted us, beaming delight to have some company. In fact when we heard he hadn't seen anyone for more than a week Jude promptly invited him to eat with us, and that pleased him so much he suggested that he drive us around to view the birds saying they were especially active at sunrise and sunset.

What an impressive excursion we had. Tommy was a wildlife expert and knew so much about the birds and other wildlife at Lake Nakuru, a caustic cauldron fringed by geysers. But even more impressive than his knowledge were the extraordinary numbers of pink flamingos that seemed to cover the lake's entire surface in a moving display of Nature at her best. Pulling up at the lake's edge didn't deter the maybe two million lesser flamingos from carrying on normal life. A medium sized bird with very red plumage they feed by bending their long necks down until their dark carmine red bills are upside down filtering out food just under the algae rich water,. Also in large numbers were greater flamingos, noticeably different with large flesh pink bills, pinkish white bodies and red wings. And we didn't have to drive far to find a large flock of great white pelicans, huge birds with three meter wingspans. In the setting sun they seemed to glow sparkling bright against the surrounding hills' dull shadows. Along the shore, wading in the shallows were African spoonbills and the much smaller pied avocet, a striking white wader with bold black markings. They constantly let out a far-carrying, melodious "kluit kluit." Flying over us in magical formations we saw lots of the much larger yellow billed stork, their plumage mainly pinkish-white with black wings and tail. A red band around their eyes flows into a blunt yellow bill that is curved at the tip, perfect pincers to grip their prey.

David was a camera buff and so were Judith and I. In the States before flying off to be wed we had purchased a Canon camera with a standard and mid-range telephoto lens. To this we had added a long barrelled 400 mm telephoto lens to capture more distant wildlife.

Next day before setting off we did another circuit and this time encountered our first water buffalo. They were massive compared to the petite and graceful Thompson gazelles.

From Nakuru we drove directly to Nanyuki at the base of Mt. Kenya, arriving at the lodge mid-afternoon. Here we spoke with a guide who told us that the next day he'd be picking up a party of walkers at the end of the road, which he said ended at about 3,000 metres. When we asked if we had to have a guide, he said no and if we liked, he'd take us up in his Land Rover when he went to fetch the lodge's guests. Naturally we agreed and said we'd take our vehicle up as high up as she'd go. That way we wouldn't have to walk so far when coming down.

Mt. Kenya - 26, 27, 28 March

Our camp in the forest at the base of Mt. Kenya somewhat startled all of us when we found great clumps of elephant poo in the clearing. There's nothing like finding poo as tall as the truck's tyre to make your hair stand on end. Jude and I slept in our tent, but when we heard trumpeting during the evening, we moved inside and slept unmolested until dawn.

After breakfast, we set off driving up through the forest and the higher we climbed the more sluggish the Bedford got. The track didn't just go up a steady incline. There were also dips that we'd have to climb out of when leaving. Every time the van barely climbed out of one, alarm bells rang and we chattered nervously about the possibility of getting stuck forever. At about 2,400 metres, after a particular sluggish climb, David pulled over to a collective sigh of relief.

With our gear in make-shift carryalls and sleeping bags slung over our shoulders, we set out along the track, climbing through thick tall forest and past even more, still steaming, elephant poo that made us a wee bit nervous. When nearly noon we heard the high revs of an engine and thought, "none too soon." But drat, a new guide was driving and he whizzed right past us without even a wave. Uh Oh! We'd been counting on that ride. Knowing that the first hut was at 4,000 metres had us put a spurt on but it wasn't enough and we were overtaken by darkness, and forced to sleep out on tundra. Miserable, I wrote in my diary.

None of us boys slept well. Jude, having been a nurse, could just about sleep standing up. But the high altitude was beginning to affect us all. Mind the beauty of the place made the discomfort a minor annoyance for me. The forest gave way to small scrubs much like waist high tea-tree, snarly and sharp. Higher up the valley these gave way to massive succulents taller than us and grasses that revealed Mt. Kenya's majestic angular rock peaks highlighted by dabs of snow like dribbled white icing in their protected clefts. As we trudged along, our breathing rate increased, not only from the exertion but also from the shortage of oxygen in the air. Meanwhile the morning's clear sky clouded, giving us added incentive for fast passage. By afternoon snowflakes fluttered down, bringing horrible thoughts of sleeping out again without protection. Late in the day, thankfully a shiny tin shed hove into view and completely fagged but delighted we rushed inside to claim basic bunks from the eight in the empty shed. Charles and Stewart were badly affected with altitude sickness. Even worse, Charles had several bad blisters from ill-fitting boots. That night a snowstorm shook the shed. We were all very cold. In the morning Charles had turned green.

Next day the three able bodies walked along the valley to the base of the peaks. Realizing we hadn't the proper gear for making an assault, we snapped a few photos then turned back. Never mind. We had given it a good try and in the process had witnessed first hand the extraordinary beauty of high altitude mountains.

From there our adventurous band made a quick stop in Nairobi to pick up more supplies, leaving the same day. After so much open space, big crowed cities were rather daunting and Nairobi didn't have the same appeal as exploring the Rift Valley where David had a mate working on a lodge under construction on the open savannah of the Maasai Mara. Driving across the semi arid land we caught our first sight of some Maasai, uniquely beautiful semi-nomadic people, who surprisingly have occupied this land for only a few hundred years. According to the fact sheets we'd obtained in Kenya's capital city, the Maasai originally inhabited the lower Nile Valley north of Lake Turkana in the northeast and began migrating south around the 15th century. Tall, fierce warriors, they moved down the long trunk of the Rift valley as far as central Tanzania between the 17th and late 18th century. Many other ethnic groups in the region were forcibly displaced, while others were assimilated into Maasai society. While going past their unusual stick huts that were arranged in a circular fashion Charles read from the literature. "The Maasai live in *kraals*. The fence around the kraal is made of thorny acacia bush which prevent lions from attacking them and their cattle……." Furthermore we learned, "It is the man's responsibility to fence the kraal, while the women construct the houses."

I have no notes on whether we had to pay to enter the game reserve, Judith doesn't think so, but we both recall driving along a dirt track across open yellow grass plains with an odd bare timber structure rising from it. It took very little time to locate Dave's friend amongst the few white workers, and after introductions were made, he asked if we wanted to see a pack of hyenas that lived close by. Personally I would have been more intrigued to see a big cat, but any tour was not to be missed, so gladly climbed inside his large seven-seat 4WD. Gosh! How surprised we were when he pulled up right alongside a sandy burrow topped by a few thorny looking bushes, and out popped the cutest little pup. Of course we didn't get out. It might have looked like it could be given a cuddle and a scratch of its head, but this was Africa where critters survive by eating other critters. Soon the pup's brothers and sisters came out to investigate the attraction, but they soon got bored sniffing the air and snuggled up together around their burrow. They lay there semi-comatose until instantly all jumped up to attention. Dave's mate said the parent must be coming and when looking about, I had just a second to snap a photo of momma returning with a lump of some animal hanging out her mouth. Hyenas are scavengers, but they also hunt in packs. They have powerful jaws, capable of cracking bone, and are not shy creatures we were soon to find out.

Kenya's countryside is varied. There are both sharp and well worn mountains, rushing rivers that run dry, and wide grasslands open to the far horizons. The largest savannah lies around Maasai Mara. It runs for miles with flat, thinly grassed land dotted with thorny trees and crisscrossed with seasonal rivulets. The Maasai Mara ecosystem holds one of the highest lion densities in the world and is where over two million wildebeest, zebra, and Thomson's gazelle migrate annually. When it was originally established as a wildlife sanctuary in 1961, the Mara covered only 520 square kilometres (200 sq mi). This was increased to 1,510 sq km (580 sq miles) of land that rises 1,500 metres to 2,170 metres above sea level and hosts over 95 species of mammals and 570 recorded species of birds. All members of the Big Five; lion, leopard, African elephant, African buffalo, and black rhinoceros, are found in the Maasai Mara. The dryer months of December to February, and sometimes March, are good times for the Big Cats.

We spent a quiet next day around the budding resort, simply overwhelmed by the variety and numbers of colourful birds that hopped right up to take crumbs from our fingers. But with talk of big cats revving us up, we were keen to go for a wander in the Bedford. A few in the workforce were knowledgeable hunters and guides, and they suggested we head south to find the outcrop of rock where a large family of lions had their den, then carry on further south to search the dry river beds, especially the overhanging trees for black leopards. All this set our blood on the boil.

Go bush looking for game, stay out o'nite – 5th April 69

Several tracks lead across the savannah and with no other traffic we edged along using a compass while up on the roof we took turns sitting in the spare tyre, camera in hand looking for big cats. I was up there when we passed an innocuous grassy lump that gave me the fright of my life when the viewfinder through my 400 mm lens filled with the golden green eyes of an enormous male lion focused intently on my succulent body. I snapped an award winning photo then a heartbeat later was banging madly on the rooftop.

There was no shortage of lions even in the midday sun. A trio of females were lounging in the shade atop a great rock face. And I think it was then that we started to realize the perfection of the wild kingdom that's so different from our world. It is in balance, no matter how many things change. If there's plentiful food, more life is created. If conditions become harsh, less is created and more perish. There is hardly any waste.

We were fortunate to be there when food and water were plentiful. Everywhere across the yellow grass veldt we saw huge herds of wildebeest, Thomson gazelle, and zebra in their thousands. And that was pretty inspiring. Somehow to witness so much wildlife gave us a lovely feeling of contentment to be inhabitants of Earth because we could see that each creature was on its own journey. They found their own sustenance, had sex, gave birth, felt passion for their young and feared death, all under the stars, sun, and harsh conditions.

In our search for a dry river bed we lost the track but came across a mother giraffe and her son nipping tender leaves off a thorny acacia tree and watched mesmerised. With a deft tongue they could lick round the thorns to pick out leaves to eat. Meanwhile a tiny bird picked nits from their long necks.

This vast land is often called simply "The Mara" which is the Maa word meaning "Mottled." An apt description for the circles of trees, scrub, savannah, and cloud shadows that fill the area.

A long day's travel following our compass across the open land left us basically in the middle of nowhere. A modern GPS would have solved our dilemma, but not really being worried we stopped in an open place as the sun set. Jude and I put up our tent close by the van, cooked a meal, and crashed after one of our most impressive days. Shame the hyenas had to spoil our rest. They made such a scary laugh that sounded like ghouls getting ready to come to eat us. Our torch lit up a pack hovering nearby and we bolted into the van to find whatever rest we could in the airlessness of five behind closed doors.

Determined to find a leopard, the pack of four amigos looking after straight talking Jude carried on, finding more herds of wildebeest, gazelles, and zebra, but nary a sight of leopard. Not a worry, we did drive right up to a pair of cheetahs prancing along in the open.

Since the lodge the Bedford had recorded 200 kilometres, and, admittedly we were lost. Fatigued, dirty and spent, imagine our joy when late that second day we came across a dirt track. But here started another trial.

Following the track we came up to a precipice where far below spread a plain as far as our eyes could see. At first what appeared to be cloud shadows, through our telephoto lens proved to be immense pools of creatures. "Surprise! Surprise! Ngorongoro Crater," Jude chimed and we suddenly realized we'd unknowingly crossed into Tanzania. Making haste under a fast sinking sun, we came upon another track signposted Oldeani which we thought must be a town. Wary of entering anything remotely civilized we trucked on, but just a kilometre further on got stopped by a closed gate.

Two Bantu came out of a bush hut and up to the van, curiously looking us over. David, who'd been driving the whole way, just wanted out so we could camp and shouted "open the gate." But the taller man asked to see his park pass.

Park Pass? David explained that we weren't visiting the park, we were just passing through. After some discussion between the guards, they told David that without a pass they would not open the gate to let us out. Hmm, what a dilemma. Maybe we were just tired, but we decided that if they wouldn't let us out, we'd camp right there at the gate. I was thinking that if we bombarded the men with requests, they'd send us packing. So asking where we could get some water I followed that up with where was the toilet. And Jude wanted to know where she could get some wood to cook dinner.

Just as the day began to cool and the intense light began to ease, a battered Land Rover drove up and a chunky, plainly dressed African swaggered up demanding to see our passports. David asked him who he was, and when he told us he was the police chief, I asked him for some identification. None was forthcoming; just another demand for our passports. Charles and Stewart wanted to ease the tension and went to find theirs when David told them not to give in, and I asked him again for some ID. In answer, the man said he'd drive us to see the head ranger, and I asked. "Is he a white man?"

Something seemed not quite right. Maybe it was the way he swaggered or maybe it was his eyes, which were very bloodshot. Anyways, when he answered in the positive, I told him that David and I would go, and that the others would stay with the truck. This didn't please him either and we went back and forth in a standoff, his temperature starting to boil. Finally it was agreed that all the men would be taken to the head ranger and Judith would stay behind, locked inside the van. Judith wasn't happy about that. "You'd better not be away long," she challenged the fellow. Leaving her behind worried me immensely, but we jumped into the rover's back tray and roared off towards the small town. There was nothing much else we could do.

Pulling in behind a corrugated iron building, he walked off inside, only to return a few minutes later with about ten big black goons. You can imagine how frightened we became.

"Now I have you just where I want you," he said in deep voice thick with anger. "I begged and begged, and you wouldn't do what I wanted, so now you are my prisoners. Get down. And march into that building," and here he pointed to a mud brick building with a thatched roof and barred windows.

His army followed us in. One was in traditional dress holding a long spear. Told to stand in a line, we weren't sure if we were about to be beaten, robbed or killed with our bodies put out where the lions would find us. Flopping down behind a desk, he was taking great pleasure in his rise to power, and after confiscating our passports, ordered us to strip. I thought Charles might begin to cry as he reached up to unbutton his shirt. But I surely wasn't going to take off my clothes and angrily told the man, "No, I'm not stripping. Charles nor will you. C'mon, we've got to stand together."

A deathly silence took over the room while the man angrily eyeballed each of us one by one.

David stepped forward to explain what had happened, how we'd left Maasai Mara to look for leopards and had simply got lost. He ended by saying that if we could leave we'd report to the authorities in Arusha and sort everything out. Meanwhile the policeman's eyes began to droop. Snapping awake and shaking his head he rattled off a few commands to his gang then struggled up to swagger out with all of them, except for the tribesman holding the spear. He was left behind. Then the door locked with the finality of a Nazi death chamber.

The man's wore a panga at his side, a Swahili machete, the traditional weapon of southern Africa. Four unarmed men against a warrior scared the living bejesus out of me until I saw that the man was frightened, and I told the lads to look menacingly at him. That did it. He turned and pounded on the door and when it quickly opened he left followed again by the clunk of the lock.

We'd not eaten after a long day, and it was now getting late. David curled up on the wooden bench, the two others sat in hard chairs, and I lay down on the policeman's desk, but not before telling them that I thought the guy was high on drugs, and not to worry, he'd be straight in the morning.

A more horrible night can not be imagined, especially for me worrying about my newly wedded wife locked in a van surrounded by savages. I doubt any of us got any rest. When we saw the sun rise, I got up and paced the small room until we heard a commotion outside. Racing to the only window we saw a group coming out of a rondavel hut made from thatch. At the head of the six or eight was our man, and what blew me away, he was puffing on what obviously was a marijuana joint!

Nothing much was said after the door was unlocked and he swaggered in holding a buff envelope. His gang took up their positions at the back. Calmly he looked us over and smiled with pleasure at seeing the state of disarray we were in. "I am sending you with a guard to Aursha. There you will be dealt with by the authorities."

Jude didn't look like she'd had much sleep either when we got back to the van, but thankfully she'd not been bothered. In quick order we got underway after telling our guard to take up a position at the back, where he soon disappeared in the road dust seeping through the rear doors. But did we care? We hadn't much sympathy for him after what we'd been put through and besides we were more concerned with what would happen at Arusha. Technically we were illegally in Tanzania.

David drove slow on the rough corrugated road and we stopped midway for an extended brunch, all calculated so we'd arrive after business hours. Our plan was to stop the letter from being delivered and get our passports back by stealth, not by force. Our plan didn't work.

Driving into Arusha, the guard directed us to the police station where he got out with the scruffy envelope containing our passports. When he returned he merely instructed us to come back in the morning then simply walked away.

Arusha, Tanzania – 8,855 km in Africa – 7th April 1969

Needless to say we spent a second restless night imagining being turned back. In the morning we were all pretty brain dead, and couldn't give a hoot if they threw us out. We'd had enough of Africa. But we had one more card up our sleeves. Early, we raced to the police station to claim the envelope, telling the desk clerk that we'd left it there for safe keeping the evening before. That trick didn't work either. It seemed the envelope had already been sent over to immigration. Mixed feelings flooded through us. Firstly we felt guilt over badly treating the Oldeani policeman, followed by rage at the way we'd been treated, mixed with abject disappointment at not being able to achieve our goal of reaching South Africa.

Inside the large brown government building we found a door marked immigration and filed in to find an empty room with wooden chairs and one barred access portal. I rang the bell and looked around grimly at my friends then turned to find a bespectacled, studious man asking what he could do for me. I wasn't sure whether I should lie or tell the truth. Being rather brain dead I mentioned a buff envelope containing our passports and asked could we have them back please. The five minutes he was away seemed to be forever with my thoughts racing from being deported to facing an African jail. I prayed Judith would not be arrested.

At last another door opened. My stomach did a back flip when footsteps were heard. Any moment now we'd be handcuffed and dragged away to a cell. But that didn't happen. The thin man returned to the grill and without a word slipped our passports under it. After two days with little rest, my mental capacity locked solid. I looked at him speechless, my eyes pleading for an answer. To wit, the man said, "You can go."

What! my mind screamed as I turned and held up our passports, then swiftly we all headed for the door. Outside, amongst the din of road traffic and incessant humanity I passed back everyone's passport. Each of us amazed, with smiles that grew even greater after spying the Tanzanian entry stamp on the first blank page. We never heard another word about that incident, nor have we ever bothered to inquire.

That day we drove straight through to the coast and bathed in the transparent waters of the Indian Ocean. The relief at being free coupled with the pleasure of being washed clean for the first time since the Ubangui River in central Africa sent our spirits soaring. Almost frivolously, we set up camp amongst the sand dunes fronting the aquamarine water next to the Tanga fishing village. So relaxed, as if we had died and gone to heaven, we ate fresh fish that night, and a wonderful fruit salad. For the next couple of days we just lazed under shady coconut trees, gorging ourselves on good food and talked about little except going straight through to South Africa We'd had enough of African bureaucracy and fearing for our lives.

From the coast at Dar es Salaam we travelled on a super highway of sorts, towards the border with Zambia. We passed through Morogoro, Iringa, and Mbeya in one day and that put us at Tunduma, where we exited Tanzania on the 14th of April 1969 after being in that country only a week.

There were plenty of heavy tankers on the road to Nakonde in Zambia. We heard they carried copper from Zambia to Dar es Salaam and returned with fuel. The ports in Mozambique were much closer, but they were closed due to a war.

We drove straight through the Zambian capital of Lusaka, not at all interested in anything but getting out of dark Africa and into the safe arms of a white ruled country. Colour had nothing to do with our passion to feel safe again. It had everything to do with the rule of law, and not being a member of the group that had dominated these people for all of living memory. Obviously there was still some animosity over what some of them perceived as domination. And they were right. Although the British had established hospitals and schools open to all, and even though they had built fine roads and train systems, they had also subjugated a lot of the arable land for their own farms. And the judicial system they installed, which was based on centuries of law making, incarcerated very many more blacks than it did whites. Yes, many jobs were created, but the profits earned from that labour went into white banks or overseas, while the locals became dependent on receiving miniscule pay. During their time at the helm, hunger and dependency grew to become a normal part of African life. When the majority were given back the power to rule, often chaos and brutality closely followed. All of this was easy to blame on the old white rulers, of which we were associated with. Another reason for us to hurry, we needed to earn some money ourselves.

Back in November of 1965, Ian Smith, the white prime minister of Southern Rhodesia signed a statement adopted by the Cabinet, announcing that Rhodesia, a British territory in southern Africa that had governed itself since 1923, now regarded itself as an independent sovereign state. It was the first break from the United Kingdom by one of its colonies since the United States Declaration of Independence nearly two centuries earlier. The reasoning behind their action was that other less advanced colonies to their north had been granted independence, while Rhodesia was refused sovereignty under Britain's new ideal of "no independence before majority rule." Theirs was the culmination of a long and convoluted history of quasi independence, promises and lies, and inequality that would require several volumes to fully explain. At the time of our arrival at Livingstone near Victoria Falls, which forms the border between Zambia and Rhodesia, we simply knew Ian Smith's regime was in control and we needed to transit that country to attain our goal of reaching South Africa.

Livingstone - 19th April 1969 – 11,510 km in Africa

It was a windy but sunny, spring day when we drove over the steel arched bridge that runs parallel to the immensely powerful Victoria Falls, the Smoke that Thunders. The Zambezi was in full flood spewing an immense amount of water over a wide gash that seemed incomprehensible in length. Mist from the falls appeared like thin cloud that fell as rain upon the bridge. Driving slowly, enjoying the scenery its rumbling power made it feel as if the bridge shook. Before going to England for our wedding, while driving across Canada Jude and I stopped at Niagara Falls. That well known attraction is only half as high and much narrower, with much less water. Tiny in comparison to the "Greatest Falling Curtain of Water on the Planet," and one of the Seven Natural Wonders of the World.

Bantu immigration officials had already checked us out of Zambia, so we were in extraordinary high spirits as we entered the immigration facilities at Masue, Rhodesia. Seeing those Caucasian officials dressed in crisp, spotless, white shirts and short trousers with knee length grey socks was as if we'd stepped through a time warp. Each and every one had a gold badge and a black name tag on their shirt fronts.

At the desk, we were cordially greeted and printed forms were provided along with ball point pens to fill them out. Passport details, home address, date of birth, all the usual stuff and with every detail completed our excitement grew till we were punching each other in glee.

Jude and I, being man and wife had a slightly different form to fill in, listing both our details and countries of birth, which the man perused before moving on to David. Here I learned that David had been born in South Africa. That fact had never come up in all our time together, but it explained his clipped manner of speech. The official nodded then went on to Charles who, although he was excited to be near journey's end seemed somewhat nervous. Stewart too seemed ill at ease. Nevertheless all the forms being completed were collected and taken through a door into a single office.

Minutes later a more senior officer came out and went straight up to Charles and said. "Sorry chap. Your total lack of funds rules you out from entry." Then turning to Stewart, he repeated word for word what he'd just said. Both lads were being refused entry.

I must have gotten a bit up on my high horse. A Yank by birth, who, in those days was used to being pushy, so I spoke up. "Excuse me, but we're travelling together, so maybe we could sort of pool our money and then you can let them in. We're all on our way to South Africa to find employment."

That seemed a good solution and I felt confident, until the chief immigration officer turned and glared at me. Rustling through the forms he approached me as he gazed upon my scribbling before looking me straight in the eyes, "Mr Binder, I see your funds are lodged in a British Bank. They are unavailable here during UDI, so I shall require from you either a plane ticket home, a guarantor, or a visa for South Africa and through passage on pubic transport."

Looking at us collectively from behind the freshly varnished counter, our shoulders must have slumped as he went on. "David being South African born and the van owner is the only one we will grant entry. The rest of you will either need sufficient funds or a guarantor. But for now you must re-enter the Republic of Zambia. Good day."

Shell shocked would be mildly stating our condition when we got outside into the African sun that felt even harsher. Holding a war council, David suggested that he travel to South Africa where he would ask his uncle to act as guarantor for Charles and Stewart. Jude said she had an aunt in Durban and asked David if he could contact her for a similar guarantee.

David left us in deeply despondent moods and Charles drove us back across the magnificent steel bridge to the Zambian customs booth which was hardly bigger than a phone box. Perplexed to see us again, the two guards were none too pleased about letting us back in. But they did, grudgingly.

Not far from their booth we found some open ground near the river and set up camp. Judith and I pitched our tent a short distance from the Bedford. Eight days passed by with hippos often walking through our camp. We did lots of reading, strolled along the mighty Zambezi River, took photos, and talked to the native fishermen. They were catching the ferocious tiger fish, a large creature extremely streamlined with razor sharp interlocking teeth. Sport fishing hadn't really started back then, so the monsters they were taking on hand lines weighed upwards of ten kilos. Beautiful creatures with striped black and silver bodies culminating in a set of chompers befitting our Australian salty crocodiles.

When David returned, he had guarantees for his friends, but Jude's relative had been away on holiday. Not to be beaten, Judith and I decided to chance another border crossing with David and co, this time late at night after the normal shift.

In the early hours of April 28th we checked out of Zambia, and boy did we cop it, the guards were not happy about being woken up. With David driving us across the steel bridge again I asked, "If we get refused, will you let us hide inside your clothes closet." In answer to his question about not getting a visa chop, full of confidence I said that I would cut one from linoleum and stamp our passports myself.

Inside the well lit office there was only one officer on at 2 AM and for a second time we filled out their form. Charles and Stewart got an entry chop in their passports then somewhat sleepily the uniformed officer opened mine to stamp it too. Holding my breath while he flipped through several pages looking for an empty spot, he had the stamp poised ready to end our troubles. With my passport open at the last used page, instead of stamping it, he paused then reached under the counter for a red ledger.

"I'm sorry, Mr. Binder," he said reading some notes in the book. "You require a guarantor or a plane ticket home, or a RSA visa and transport. Do you have any of those?"

"How do you know?" I asked.

"See this stamp?" Sure I did, I'd been looking at it in my passport for over a week, working out how I could duplicate it.

"See the R/E?" And he explained that what I'd thought were the official's initials actually meant "Refused Entry!"

Back outside, the cool night air wilted my courage and I told David to carry on without us. The way our luck was running we'd probably be arrested and spend an eternity in a white run jail. Bloody Officials!

You might be able to imagine the depths of depression we felt while carrying our few belongings back across the steel bridge in the falling rain from the smoke that thunders. Even worse, after waking the Zambian guards a second time, without a vehicle they wouldn't let us back in.

Homeless and stateless, we wandered halfway back across the bridge and hid from the rain under a maintenance canopy. Chilled to the bone by the time the sun rose, a rainbow forming above the wide falls rejuvenated our determination; we'd figure out a way of badgering our way in and trudged back again towards the Zambian border. There the shift had changed, replaced by two fellows we knew, who after telling them the truth, made us a hot cup of tea while vowing retribution on the white Rhodesian officers.

That day we hitchhiked into Livingstone where I changed a traveller's cheque then we purchased some food before I placed an international telephone call to the South Africa Immigration department. Geez, as if our day hadn't been depressing enough, the two operators, one white, the other black, started shouting insults at each other. Oh please God, I prayed, get us out of here.

Once connected and my problem explained, the South African official was very helpful, offering to post a visa to me at the Livingstone Post Office. Uttering a silent thank you, I rejoined my bride, and then to kill a bit of time we put our thumbs out to hitchhike to Kariba dam, supposedly a sight worth seeing.

May Day parade at Kafue saw the main street filled with Chinese waving Red flags aplenty. And then late that night we could have been killed. It happened while snuggled up in our tent which we'd pitched outside the local drive-in cinema so we could watch a movie without the sound. Awoken by two voices just outside. Both sounded intoxicated. They were arguing about how they would slit our white throats then take our money. We hardly let out a breath. Fortunately the most vociferous reasoned we were only poor white trash living on the streets and not worth killing.

We planned on buying a third class train ticket from Livingstone to Beitbridge, the border with South Africa, just like the official had demanded - a visa and through transport. So we went back to Livingstone a week later, finding the visa had not arrived. Presenting myself at the Post Office the next day, again nothing under the letter B. Facing the prospect of finding another day's camp and feeling depressed I turned to go out and noticed that there wasn't much mail in the pigeonholes, but there was one envelope under the letter J. So I asked the lady to look at that one. Bingo! Filed under J for Jack, my South African visa had been there three days.

Visa arrives 7th of May 1969

Having noticed a train waiting we rushed to the station next door, where I requested two one way tickets, third class to Beitbridge, a journey of some thirty-six hours. "Surely you mean first class," the rather sceptical lady kept asking. Shaking my head, I paid just a few dollars and clutching Judith's arm we ran down the length of carriages, passing First Class with gold lettering, then a few Second Class until at last we came to a long line of shabby carriages with heavy black Third Class signs. The rows of hard timber benches inside were pretty well packed with a mixture of all sorts of poor workers, village women, babes in arms and curious kids, even a few men in poor quality suits. And the floor was piled high with woven baskets of food and clothes, including some poultry clucking on top. Of course we stuck out like albinos. Never mind. The train gave a hoot and slowly hissed off for the promise land. Once the train got going our relief became palpable, the faces around us turned from astonishment to big grins as we settled in. Livingston soon slipped behind, replaced by the muddy rushing waters of the Zambezi.

Crossing the bridge into Rhodesia for the third time, Jude snuggled close in my arms as we chuckled, whispering about beating all obstacles that had barred attaining our goal. And our mood grew in jubilance with each clatter of the rails, right up to the moment a dapper red capped Negro conductor entered our cattle car. His manner turned to one of shock, almost fright, when his eyes caught sight of our pale skin and without hesitation he was upon us.

"Quickly mam, sir. You get straight away up to second class!" He exclaimed pointing forward.

"But. But," I stammered, "We haven't the extra fare."

"Sorry sah. No arguments! Get. Do you have any idea what will happen at the next station?"

His expression insisted we be fully obedient and moments later Judith and I were opening a second class suite as the train slowed into the Masue train station. We were so delighted at what we saw, our flushed smiles would have matched the plush red leather seats that made into beds. There was even a pull down stainless washbasin with water taps. Thinking of the wonderful comfort before us Judith threw up her arms in happy disbelief then cuddling each other we watched the station siding slide past through the windows, filled shoulder to shoulder with humanity, pushing and jostling ready to fill third class.

Moments later came a gentle knock at the door and a white uniformed official smiled as he entered and handed us the forms that we'd filled in twice before. It took less than a minute to do that familiar chore and hand them back with our passports. Our long journey down the dark African continent seemed on the point of completion and so I gave my lover a reassuring hug, just as the officer cleared his throat.

"I am very sorry but I see that you have been refused entry and I will have to ask you to detrain." His words bombarded our ears like enemy shellfire.

As if hit by a cat of nine tails, Jude exploded into wailing and made such a scene stomping her feet while my anger grew white hot before it exploded. "You can't do that! We've done everything demanded of us."

He was extremely apologetic, and we could see the sympathy showing through his eyes. But he insisted. And so we gathered up our few belongings, took one last look at the plush cabin and walked off the train to the confused looks from our helpful conductor. Then as Jude sobbed uncontrollable, the train rumbled slowly on its way.

In the official's government car we were chauffeured to the familiar border station where hardly waiting for it to stop, I rushed into the Chief's office and began a loud tirade.

"You said if we got through tickets to South Africa and I got a visa you'd let us in! So what's going on?" I shouted shaking my fists.

Withstanding as much as he could, quite calm but stern, he said quietly, "One more word Mr. Binder and you'll go back across that bridge."

I shut my mouth and stared angrily. Jude was still weeping outside when he called in the other officer, and although I didn't hear what was said, his tone of annoyance came clearly through the closed door.

Re-entering his chamber, I was told he was considering issuing us a three day transit visa. I fumed again saying he'd taken away our paid transport and that now we were stuck.

"Mr. Binder, without making any promises we will try to organize transport with someone going towards Bulawayo. But this is a quiet station and I cannot say when that might be."

Shortly afterwards, while sitting on the outside bench reviewing our sudden change of plans, the shift changed and one of the departing officers came to invite us to stay at his place. I think that one act of kindness broke the drought. We stayed overnight with Greg, second in command, enjoying our first hot showers since leaving England, followed by what can only be described as a succulent meal served by servants on a table covered with a fresh tablecloth, and then we slept in bed for the first time in five months.

From there our story gets better and better. Next day Greg drove us into work and almost straight away arranged a ride with a French merchant travelling to Bulawayo. Can't say we conversed hugely on the ride through vacant countryside upon the first strip roads we'd encountered. Strip roads are two parallel strips of bitumen laid over a dirt track. Approaching Bulawayo the countryside began to green up with small patches of forest interspersed with agriculture, which opened onto the town's first roundabout, where the Frenchman pulled over and let us out, and wished us good luck. Supposedly we had two more days to legally transit the country, but I was far more worried about getting into South Africa after the trouble at Victoria Falls.

There was little traffic, in fact none the next few hours, but as the day began to cool a lone vehicle pulled up and a man asked, "What are you doing out here on the side of the road?"

A brief account of our last few weeks saw his face twist and drop. "Can't have you two adventurers getting into trouble, can we? Get in." As it happened we not only secured a ride, but also a bed for the night.

Entering a small dusty property, an enclosed lush veggie patch down the side of a simple, bungalow with a tinned roof came into view. Rather stiff from our full day sitting in the Frenchman's Ute, we got out slowly as a slim lady opened the front door. As soon as she greeted us, Jude's eyes lit up.

"Ay well," Jude twanged in her native Geordie lilt. "And where would you be coming from?" her face lit by a broad smile.

Right on the doorstep in the last golden glow from the sun, Anne embraced Judith then pushed her away to arm's length. "Ay, I'm Anne from Sunderland, and who might you be?"

Sunderland is just a stone's throw from where Judith was born, where she had lived all her life before meeting me. An avalanche of high pitched laughs followed one after another while we boys stood back, tears in my eyes seeing my wife so at home and happy. In rapid fire, we learned that Anne had also trained as a nurse, at the other major hospital just over the river from where Judith had trained at the Royal.

Richard had been born in Kenya, where he'd lived until recently. He met Anne when on vacation in Britain and together they had returned to East Africa, where he repaired farm machinery. But with Kenya gaining its independence, the systems he'd come to expect began to fail and their quality of life dropped, not wanting to leave Africa, they decided to move south to begin life together in Ian Smith's Rhodesia.

All that evening we told stories of travelling overland through a continent ripped apart by wars and upheavals created by rapid change. For most of our story telling, Anne sat next to my lady, first transfixed at the dangers we'd faced, then consoling with cuddles when hearing Jude talk about our hardship and lack of hygiene. On the positive side we told of our exposure to the wild kingdom and how observing the other creatures had affected us deeply. For two who had lived surrounded by manmade buildings, lights, and roads, to be out under the heavens, reliant upon our wit and resources had bonded us firmly to Earth. Our eyes had been opened to its majesty causing us to wonder whether the human phenomena wasn't racing away from a much better future, one synchronised with Earth, the creator of all life. In sharing our stories with these folk, we realized just how self-reliant we had become. By overcoming one hardship, then another, and another, building our confidence up bit by bit we had achieved difficult, dangerous, tasks. Little could we know that gaining those skills and convictions would one day lead us to take on much greater challenges.

When we related our horror stories caused by our lack of funds, Richard suggested we find employment in Bulawayo, saying there was heaps of work available for a talented man.

I was very worried about gaining entry into South Africa, and so when talk of jobs and residency came up, we agreed to pursue the matter. Next day Richard took me to the immigration office, where a few phone calls secured a job interview with a steel fabricator who needed shop drawings prepared, and that very same afternoon, May 10th 1969, we were sworn in as residents of Rhodesia, now called Zimbabwe. Secretly we were not serious about staying. Primarily because under the sanctions imposed by the UN for Ian Smith's Unified Declaration of Independence (UDI), the money earned in Rhodesia was valueless outside the country. But I figured if the South Africans wanted us to have funds enough to get back home, we'd have enough for a ride to Bulawayo.

Desperate people do desperate things. And you can imagine after so many upsets and roadblocks, when this close to our goal, I was not going to let anything stop us from reaching it. But even way back then, I had a creed. I would never physically hurt any other person or prevent them from perusing their goals as long as they didn't hurt others too. My course of action seemed to fit that guide, so we told everyone we'd be travelling to RSA to pick up our baggage, and set off hitchhiking to Beitbridge, where without one hiccup we entered South Africa on the 14th of May 1969.

Ceuta, North Africa to Johannesburg, 12,720 km in a five month African Honeymoon.

Reflections in a Sailor's Eyes

My Dad loved fishing

Dad, my sister Diane and me, age 12

FAILED AGAIN

Failure is a word that can strike despair in many young minds. And yet, now that I am older I'm proud to admit that I've failed several times. My first failure when a young boy was a boat I built which simply wouldn't float. It was supposed to be fast, so I thought it had to be sleek and narrow. But while sketching its design, I realized I'd never built anything. Never used fibreglass, never made a form, nor knew anything about sailing. But building that boat changed my life forever.

I remember traipsing back from the beach late one day and passing two large open doors where a great hubbub was erupting from the room's smoke filled interior. Peeking in, men were shouting, and a fellow at the front was waving a wooden hammer as if stirring a hornet's nest. For awhile I watched amused, and then became transfixed by a rough timber box banged down upon the auctioneer's desk.

"What will you bid for this mystery box?" the auctioneer called to the crowd who laughed while a few elbowed their mates.

I had seen boxes like that in my storybooks and knew lost treasure could be in them. So when the man at the front called for bids, from the back, I blurted out, "A dollar! I'll give a dollar for that box."

Heads turned and searched the room. Those around me looked down and emitted a chuckle. One slender old man gave me a wink and called out, "The boy bids a dollar." And again the room buzzed like that hornet's nest had been given a kick.

When I brought that trunk home and opened it up, it wasn't filled with old treasure – no gold or pieces of eight. In fact, it contained nothing more than a loose roll of smelly, stiff cloth that was tarnished off-white with a rope sewn around its edge. Then as I pulled it out, I recognized it as a ship's sail.

Fingering the coarse cloth with my soft little hands sent my mind wandering. Where had this sail been? I wondered. Maybe to the far side of the ocean that stretched away from the end of my street. And in my mind I saw a ship sail past the pyramids of Egypt. Maybe this sail had cruised along a coconut coast with wooden dhows manned by dusky men.

Or had it sailed around the world and withstood vicious storms? Fingering a ragged hole I was sure that was so. Then and there I decided to build my own little ship so my tarnished white sail could fly in the wind once again.

As I said, I didn't know anything about making boats. So I started by looking through all my books, and from what I could see, that fibreglass material was the best stuff. With my father's hammer and some of his nails, a few burlap sacks and a big bag of plaster lugged back from the hardware shop, I built myself a form. But gosh, it had more ripples than swells on the ocean. That didn't matter. There were more problems to come. Like applying the fibreglass material, which proved kind of tricky. More than half ended up on our garage floor. That didn't matter either. My poppa never barked. He just watched over me with a great big smile. You see, he was just as keen, and knew just as little.

Then the big day arrived. Father and son took their new boat down to the beach, where surrounded by a big crowd, she was dragged into the surf. Pity my poor pop, he couldn't swim a stroke, and yet he stood neck deep in the frothy stuff, pushing his son and his lop-sided boat out to sea. Bit of a shame it wouldn't stay afloat.

If there's one thing good about failing, it's that we learn what doesn't work. So you see, from that first major defeat I realized I never knew why things float. I never knew about displacement. So, from that one failure, I learned heaps.

Failed Again

Reflections in a Sailor's Eyes

1986 Entering Coffs Harbour, completing world circumnavigation

BANYANDAH

A Hartley South Seas - uniquely different from the water line up

Now our boat ain't worth a lot of money, but she's been 'round the world. Bless her. And she's sailed across the North Pacific as well with snow falling on her decks, buried her masts underwater on that trip. Poor baby. She took that better than us, just as she did crossing the Great Australian Bight one frosty winter when mile high swells swept us off our feet and took cargo ships from our sight. She's a strong little lady, all 38 feet and 12 tonnes of her.

Born in a Sydney backyard that looked upon the Opera House when it was being constructed, she's homebuilt, and became our family's first home immediately after touching the sea at Berry's Bay in 1973. Our mate named her *Banyandah* from a book of nice sounding Northern Territory Aboriginal words. It means *'Home on the water,'* and that's what she became; our home on the water for fifteen years as our two sons grew into men while we travelled this good Earth seeking adventure and wisdom.

Banyandah didn't cost much to build. We didn't have much after buying nappies and the usual baby stuff. But that was okay because when we took our babies to see pretty corals and fishes on the Great Barrier Reef, we already knew how to survive on next to nothing. And that's all we had; a good boat, some fishing gear and a big bag of rice.

Funny thing is we didn't know how to sail the craft we'd just built. Calamity Jane had nothing on us. Crikey, I once swore a blue streak while clinging for dear life atop the masthead while trying to figure out what a strange bright light was, low and close to the setting sun. Couldn't navigate either. Too busy building the darn thing to learn. Figured we'd have time enough once underway. And besides, thought it couldn't be that hard. Other folk had been doing it for years. But now that more than a hundred thousand sea miles have passed us by, we think you'd better be far cleverer and darn lucky to get away with those sorts of thoughts because the sea can be mighty unkindly. Beautiful, yes. Awesome too.

But a place where your spirit will be tested. And if you're found wanting, then God forbid, you endanger your fellow man unnecessarily. We read before getting into this business that true sailors never leave port unless prepared to look after themselves. We believe that's a truism lost on some of today's fair-weather bred. So when preparing for sea, forget you've got a mobile phone, an HF, or an EPIRB, and remember you're a sailor in a long line of folk who dotted their i's and crossed their t's, and then went out to look after themselves.

The first item needed to take care of you is a good seaworthy ship. That sums up *Banyandah*. Long keel, decent draft, full forefoot, easily handled rig made of stout gear with solid handrails to keep us on board. Her accommodation is split by a roomy, well-protected cockpit that contains only basic instrumentation. Nothing conspicuous that'll attract thieves; just depth sounder, speed, and two engine gauges plus a trusty Saura compass that we've had right from the beginning. Our radios and GPS are unobtrusively below. Under her cockpit sits the diesel that made Perkins famous. Robust, yet simple to repair anywhere in the world; it delivers an honest 70 horsepower to her 50 cm three bladed propeller through a 2:1 mechanical gearbox that's controlled via a lever we simply nudge for a few revs, fore or aft, to ease us into the tightest spots. Up forward, below a flush deck so large we've held slumber parties of ten, is a galley to starboard and settee that converts into a double bed to port. Then there's our loo, which we boast has a hot shower and homemade Lavac style dunny that's uncloggable. It can be diverted into a sump for in-port use. Opposite that there's another seat, then through a fancy doorway trimmed in silver ash, a double vee berth forward cabin. Aft of the cockpit is our domain. As I used to say to the tourists we once took on overnighters, "You can sleep anywhere, but not in that double bed." It's in a huge cabin with our nav station, electrical panel, and clothes drawers. It's cosy. Panelled in Aussie Red Cedar with Scented Rosewood trim, it features full headroom above floor panels of cork. We've learnt from hard years of scraping back faded, peeling varnish that polished timber survives best below decks. So above decks, where timber is exposed, we've used only durable timbers; teak, qwila, and a bit of *Toona Australis* trimming the dodger.

Banyandah is a very practical sea boat. Her roller furling headsail comes off the end of a short bowsprit that keeps her anchor away from her topsides. Then we have a hanked-on staysail that saved us a bit of money and the extra windage when tacking the headsail around. Her mainmast carries a slab reefed high-aspect sail that goes aloft on Dacron halyards around a winch with base handles permanently attached. And at the bow sits our workhorse 1200 Maxwell anchor winch that quickly brings up the 20 kg CQR on 70 metres of 10mm chain that we almost always put all out. Two handy footswitches lets me easily direct Jude with a raised arm, so she can drive right up to our hook while I pick it up.

Banyandah's so suited to travelling the oceans of Earth, yet she's hardly worth what her gear cost. Why? Well she's one of those ferrocement gals. Yep, lots of mesh and 6 mm rods, all filled up with cement - just add ten thousand hours of hard yakka. We raised our sons aboard her while visiting about every culture and continent. We fished, dove, and sailed our way to most of the world's top spots, battled the Red Sea, immersed ourselves in Europe, stood in wonder under the statues on Easter Island, and marvelled at Nature in the Galapagos. After all that, *Banyandah* was rather tired. The boys and a hundred thousand sea miles had taken their toll. So, as it was time to get the kids away on their own path, we plucked her out the briny and stood her at the front of our lot.

The years that followed were kind to Miss B. We had a wood shop during that time, so when a decision had to be made whether to dig a big hole to bury our lady or cut a hole in her for steps up to a museum, we elected to refit her for our later years. Everything came out; cupboards, valves, wiring, everything back to bare hull. Well, you know how it is. Best laid plans and all that. Five years became ten, then fifteen. *Banyandah* stood patiently, passer-bys tooted, while we, her builders aged too. But the day came when everything important found its place. On our thirty-eighth wedding anniversary we took the decision to refloat the old girl for a quick spin around Australia to see if we could both cut the mustard.

All up, it took sixteen years to rebuild our home on the water. Now she's all new, except her hull. Sure wish we could say that for her owners.

Reflections in a Sailor's Eyes

Amboyna Cay - Spratly Islands
South China Sea
Occupied by North Vietnamese - 1979

Victory! in Brunei

RUNNING SCARED AT SPRATLY

Back in 1979, the world had no satellites guiding our every movement day and night. Instead, all ships used the heavens to navigate, and our maps, what we called charts, were sometimes inaccurate – some had been made by aerial surveillance during WWII with soundings dating back to the earliest explorers.

Originally published in the American Amateur Radio magazine 73

Only steel nerves and luck stood between the 1979 Amateur Radio expedition and disaster. From the log of the *Banyandah* - South China Sea, March 31, 1979

0600 Dawn is breaking on this our third day at sea since departing Brunei, North Borneo. On the far eastern horizon an expanding band of changing pastels is rising. The sea and sky are becoming distinct.

As the sky brightens, pearl-grey clouds become highlighted with crowns of liquid gold and a charge of excitement builds through all on board. Silhouetted against this display of Nature's beauty, my six passengers are scanning the horizon for the first hint of our mysterious destination. Their chatter like a flock of birds greeting a new day.

Somewhere ahead lays Amboyna Cay in the Spratly Islands. According to the pilot book, we should find only a 50 m patch of sand surrounded by a bit of fringing reef. But recent hostile military activity in this area may have changed all of that.

0700 According to my sights and calculations we should be very close and I'm going to climb to the masthead for a look round.

0715 From the top, a tiny irregularity breaks the otherwise barren horizon and elated, I yell down, "Land ho!" This raises a cheer from the deck and happy excited faces turn to follow the direction of my outstretched arm.

Nothing can be seen from deck level so a barrage of questions assaults me as I climb down *Banyandah*'s 15 m main mast. "How big is it?" "Is it sand?" "Any trees?" "Did you see any buildings?"

"Hold on guys. It's just a blip. In a half-hour it'll pop out the ocean as if by magic."

0745 Through binoculars, a yellowish sand crescent is just visible, rising out the sea as we ride up the swell, disappearing as we slid down. Everybody wants a look through the glasses, but Harry Mead, VK2BJL, team leader, and a new friend soon to become a dear and significant person in our lives gets the first chance.

"Jack, is that a rock I see on the right-hand side?" Harry asked in his slow half-laugh half-lisp handing back the glasses, and as *Banyandah* rose on a larger swell I saw what could be a rock, a wreck, almost anything. It's just too small to make out.

0800 It's not a rock or a wreck. It now looks like a huge tent – like a circus tent, only all tan in colour. Other objects, possibly structures, are situated about it. I'm beginning to get worried. The guys are getting edgy too. Stew, K4SMX, keeps talking about a letter he has which explains that we are a scientific expedition studying radio propagation. He keeps saying the letter is written in both Russian and Vietnamese. That sounds like he knows something I do not.

0810 There are three distinct groups of people visible on that tiny mound of sand, a group at each end with a smaller number on the top. The "top" hardly more than two metres above the sea.

0815 The smaller centralized group has begun signalling us with semaphore flags and everyone turns to me.

John, KV4KV, asks the obvious, "What are they saying?"

"Look, I haven't a clue," I said a bit perplexed. "But I think I'll anchor just offshore and row in for a friendly chat. After all, we don't even know who they are and they can only tell us to go away, right?"

My wife doesn't look so sure, but the others nod or mumble comments like, "We've come this far, we ought to give it a go."

After everyone agrees, Stew beams another of his southern hospitality smiles and says, "I'll even go in with you."

0915 Trouble! We're running scared, powering away from Amboyna Cay just as fast as our 70 hp engine will push us. And we're searching the horizon in every direction for any intruder, deathly frightened we might sight one.

What happened back there was insane. I mean, we're just ordinary folk – peaceful family men – out on an adventure. We meant them no harm, and there was definitely no reason for them to try to kill us.

I guess things really began to happen once we came within a mile of the island. From that distance we could see that the cay was about half the size of a football field with several buildings of clapboard and corrugated iron at the centre, two radio towers as well. We could also see that the perimeter was reinforced with a wall of sandbags, and the wall facing us had a sign in large white letters BAOTHEP.

We began our final approach with one operator at the radio, scanning the bands, listening for a possible contact with the island. The other ham operators were on deck, clustered close together by the centre cockpit where Judith was at the controls, and I was at the bow searching for a clear patch in the coral to drop the anchor.

I remember it became deathly quiet – only distant sounds of a light wind upon the sea and the sound of my heart beating in my ears pumping adrenaline through my body. As I reached for the anchor release, an abrupt order rang out on the cay and groups of green-clad men began to scatter.

Explosions cut the air – boom…boom…boom…boom. The physical impact of the concussion slammed into us. Thrown to the deck, my mind began recording every detail of those hour-long seconds.

I saw four puffs of grey-white smoke hanging in mid-air above the cay and heard a shrill whistle overhead, then felt heat on my cheeks. The five Amateur operators, heedless of injury, threw themselves headlong into my cockpit. Hardly comprehending that our lives were in danger, I looked back along the deck and saw the two drums of petrol nakedly lashed to the rails and instantly my mind's eye imagined a huge orange death ball of fire erupting from them and screamed, "Move it! Move it! Full power!"

Getting up on all fours, I saw Judith at the helm, kicking bodies away from the floor mounted gearbox control. And then with her eyes sunk deep and her teeth exposing a grin of animal fear, she slammed the boat into forward gear and pushed the throttle to full power.

Reflections in a Sailor's Eyes

For what seemed hours, we waited, unmoving, rigid, our every nerve straining for the slightest warning of a new attack. But none came. We were lucky.

Directly after the attack we returned to Brunei. Three expedition members thought it too dangerous to continue. Secretly so did I. Docking at Maura Port in the early morning hours after six days at sea, Harry, Stew, and Bill wanted to try again. A new island was chosen, one which US government officials assured us was "safe." That assurance reinstated my confidence, and I accepted the charter. Later those assurances proved nothing more than hog-wash.

We re-provisioned that day and departed that night. Two and a half days later, on a morning very similar to the one at Amboyna, we made landfall. Immediately two unmarked ships closed in on us from opposite directions. One steamed directly across our bow only 200 m off. It appeared to be a phantom ship – no flag, no markings, and no crew visible. When it had passed, we reversed our course, put on power, and each of us silently prayed.

Again, we were lucky. But all of us thought we had just about used up our quota of good luck. Tired and fed up with being scared all the time, we decided to head for home. That night, dear Harry questioned me so sweetly over where we might go, another sand island perhaps, that I changed course for a reef charted as completely submerged. It was near our course line and worth investigating.

Arriving the next morning, a hot glassy-smooth day with absolutely no wind or swell, as we rounded the weather end, I watched from the masthead and shook my head in disbelief. Our luck was still holding. Right on the reef edge, a cluster of coral rocks had been dashed up by some long ago storm and a baby sand island was forming. It was no larger than my foredeck, but appeared to stay above water at all tides.

That tiny scrap of sand, surrounded by miles of open ocean and hostile forces, became 1S1DX, the last active amateur radio station in the Spratly Islands. In four days of operations, 30,000 contacts were made from that dollop of sand. A great result for the team.

Footnote:

Sadly, four years later, a Singapore yacht operated by the owner and his wife, carrying four German hams on a similar radio expedition to Amboyna Cay in the Spratly Group, was fired upon by Vietnamese forces. One German radio operator perished immediately when the yacht burst into flames. The rest of the party drifted for ten days on debris, with a second operator dying of thirst the day before the others were rescued by a passing Japanese freighter. This tragedy should never have happened as the attack on *Banyandah* had been widely reported.

My comment on this today:

Obviously I was naive not to think of the oil in that area. Brunei, one of the richest in the world at that time, derived its wealth from offshore petroleum. The Vietnam conflict had only just ended and they were SE Asia's most powerful force and one of the five Nations claiming the Spratly Island region. From what I remember, the team's friend at the CIA gave us inaccurate information because the CIA never thought we'd really go.

The area is notoriously rich in oil and natural gas deposits; however, the estimates vary greatly. The Republic of China estimates that the South China Sea may contain 17.7 billion tons of crude oil (compared to Kuwait's 13 billion tons). Therefore even today the islands and reefs of the South China Sea are hotly disputed among several sovereign states within the region, namely Brunei, the People's Republic of China, Taiwan, Malaysia, the Philippines, and Vietnam.

Life Afloat ~ The Four J's

THE DEAD DON'T CRY
Indian Ocean 1984

The closest planet to the sun could not be hotter than Jude standing in that airless room, staring at a bead of sweat sliding round and round a tight black curl, following it until a droplet formed. Falling onto a black neck, it joined others further staining the man's white collar.

A new droplet starting its journey sent Jude's fingers up through her own blonde strands and finding them wet, she mechanically lifted them from her neck, releasing a trickle of sweat, and that started alarm bells ringing.

Finding it difficult to focus, she followed its run down her arm until discovering wetness darkening the envelope containing her children's schoolwork released a sigh, followed by a deep groan. Shaking her head, she wondered whether stamps would stick to such a soggy envelope.

"Avez-vous parlé?"

The odd sound vaguely penetrates Jude's haze and looking up as if touched by a zephyr whispering across a flat ocean, two piercing mocha brown eyes demand her attention. Her brain still drowning in cement, instead of responding, she knits her brows.

"I asked if you spoke," said the gentleman who had turned in the queue. His clipped cultured voice had produced an exotic sound, and curiosity went to work like dynamite, and she explodes. "Where do you come from?"

From out a pink cavern rimmed in snow white, the young man laughed, maybe a bit too loudly. Recovering his composure, he announces, "I am Malagasy. From the island of Madagascar. Have you been there?"

Madagascar! Jude loved the sound and tried to roll it off her tongue as easily as the stranger, and repeated, "Madagascar." The sound igniting visions of green mountains and primitive people.

Her first try half-whispered, she said louder, "Madagascar." This time the sound flowed with the rolling of lips and darting tongue.

A puzzled, slow shake of her head at last brought the man his answer. "Err, no, I've never been there." And her smile extended the full width of her face. "But I live on a boat and could go there."

Somewhat unbalanced by her response, the black man steadied his weight as his eyes re-appraised the lady in a sarong that clung to her curves. Vainly he tried to visualise what she had meant, but not getting any images, he asked for a clue. "Boat?" he prompted.

"It's a yacht, actually. I'm with my husband and two children on a ketch lying in the main port."

Grappling with the aberrant image, he asked again, "Children? On a boat?"

"Yes, my sons; one's twelve, the other's thirteen. We're leaving Mauritius in a few days, sailing for Mombasa. What about you?"

Her question echoed around the cramped Port Louis Post Office, causing a few heads to turn while the black stranger continued to have difficulty conjuring up a vision of a family afloat. Silent moments passed until no longer able to resist the excitement beaming out the woman's eyes, he began.

"Please, you must pardon me. My name is Felicieu. Normally I am a student in Paris, but tomorrow I fly to Diego Suarez to visit my mother."

More exotic sounds from the young man's lips tightened her belly with anticipation. Never having met anyone from Madagascar inflamed her thirst to know more, and wanting her children and husband to meet this man, she blurted out, "Would you like to see my boat?"

Seven hundred nautical miles separate Madagascar from the island of Mauritius, which was uninhabited when first discovered by Arab traders in 975 AD. It was also home for thousands of fat birds which could not fly and tortoises which could not run. Mauritius remained little changed until 1638 when the Netherlands East India Company set up a settlement of twenty-five colonists who exploited the island's ebony and ambergris. In the following few years, a hundred slaves were imported from Madagascar and convicts were sent from Batavia. From North Sea ports came free colonists, hardened men, settlers of desperation rather than brave idealists. Lawless years passed until one bright day in September 1715, Guillaume d'Arsel raised the French flag on a bluff overlooking what is today Port Louis, taking possession of Mauritius for King Louis XV, and naming the island, Ile-de-France.

The Dead Don't Cry

Much has changed since that day, and upon leaving the Port Louis Post Office, Judith and the tall Malagasy were engulfed by a sea of people, a virtual tidal wave of humanity; some black, chestnut, others dusky or pale, in a mix of turbans, sackcloth, and straw hats. A third is Creole, a blend of bloods, mostly poorly attired.

The two had rushed around a corner and escaped through an archway, the only opening in a wrought-iron fence topped by sharp spears meant to keep the riff-raff out of the port area which now lay before them in something like a giant boot. Down the ankle led to open sea, and on both sides, cranes squealed, and ships groaned shifting bags of sugar into their bellies. On their right, along the foot stood a continuous line of corrugated iron sheds bearing cast metal nameplates attached to flaking paint. Alongside the dock in front of these were several small cargo ships from various nations, and perhaps a dozen dhows of weathered timbers, a few ornately painted in gay colours.

This harbour had given safe haven to Abel Tasman and James Cook, and here Matthew Flinders met a terrible fate. The port has also seen a steady stream of black misery. Where broken-hearted men, taught by voodoo that demons lay across the sea, had been shipped to hell around the world in slave irons.

Ahead on the quay, next to two brown masts, a crowd of dusky dockworkers burst out laughing as they jostled each other for a better view of the craft alongside.

"Come," Jude commanded, taking Felicieu's hand before pushing into the crowd, letting her white face be her passport. From the quayside, a tidy forty footer lay upon quiet turquoise water, her cream decks smooth and unbroken except for two small hatches and a central wheelhouse. On one side lay a blood-red gumdrop shaped dinghy, and upon the other, two bronzed demons raced for a rope dangling from the masthead. The taller, a little faster, leapt and claimed possession. But the other tackled him, and both went flying as if two pearls on a string out over rippled water. At the pinnacle of their arc they dropped in unison creating a beautiful white splash which brought a delighted roar from the crowd.

"My kids," admitted Jude, feeling an odd mixture of pride and embarrassment as she tugged her visitor towards the wharf's metal ladder.

After reaching the deck, she shouted, "Jason! Jerome! Dry off and meet Felicieu." Then stomping her foot twice, she called, "Hey, Jack! Meet someone from Madagascar!"

A few seconds later, leading him through the narrow companionway, a curious wonder spread over Felicieu.

"Magnifique!" he exclaimed. "I'm surprised. Like a house, only everything is smaller. I think it's lovely."

Behind him, the doorway filled with a dripping wet Jason sporting a mischievous smile.

"Yeah, but it's not the same." Reaching down, Jason said, "I'll bet you've seen nothing like this." And he gave the two-burner stove a push which set it swinging. Before Jas could answer Felicieu's questioning look, Jude explained, "That's so I can cook at sea. When the boat tilts, the stove remains level. Otherwise, we'd have lopsided bread."

A mop of snow-white hair scrambled past Jason and alongside the tall stranger. Looking up, taking his hand, Jerome asked in an eager voice, "Would you like to see where I sleep?"

"Where WE sleep." Jason pushed forward to chide his younger brother.

Felicieu chuckled warmly at the pair. "I shared a room with my two older brothers, and sometimes, I didn't like it either." His wistful voice hinted at lost pillow fights. "But please, let me see your bedroom."

Leading him forward, Jerome corrected him. "It's not a bedroom. On boats, they're called cabins."

Slamming lockers open, two young teenagers captivated their tall, aristocratic visitor with knick-knacks collected from around the world; intricate seashells, a Buddha carved from ivory, stamps, coins, postcards. When they ran out of goodies, Jude opened a seat locker and extracted several soft-covered books, and handed them to Felicieu. "These are books I use to teach *Banyandah School*. Each contains twelve lessons," she explained. "We mail the tests back to Australia for marking."

An educated man from a remote island, Felicieu appreciated the importance of comprehensive schooling. While leafing through the material, he explained that many on Madagascar wanted to learn, but there were too few teachers and little resources. Glancing up, admiration had softened his aloof nature when he announced that this meeting had inspired him to investigate introducing a similar system to his island.

The Dead Don't Cry

Jude's small-town upbringing made her appear disarmingly charming when she asked Felicieu, "Tell us more about your island."

Rubbing his chin in thought, the expectant eagerness filling the boys' eyes touched him.

"The Malagasy people are a mixture of Africans and Asians who started arriving two thousand years ago," he began. "The first were Malay-Polynesian migrants who crossed the Indian Ocean in open boats from South East Asia. Later, Arab, Indian, and Portuguese traders arrived, and they brought slaves from eastern Africa. With them came European pirates and French colonists who mixed with the population to create the eighteen official tribes that inhabit Madagascar today."

Playful eyes engaged the boys when Felicieu whispered, "Do you know that not long ago, from bases along Madagascar's coast, over one-thousand pirates plundered ships rounding the Cape of Good Hope?"

Jerome rushed away to fetch the atlas and tossed it open on the saloon's small table. Both boys turned pages until a map appeared showing Madagascar long and thin next to the vast African continent. Felicieu pointed near the top.

"My family lives here in Diego Suarez. With a population of forty thousand, it is the north's administrative centre."

A thoughtful smile formed on his lips while he paused as if deciding whether to continue. Then he announced, "My mother is the elected government representative." His smile straightened. "But she's a member of the opposition party. And that's a big problem with today's Marxist government."

On the map, Jude put her finger on Diego Suarez, sitting as if by fate, very close to our route to Africa. After mentioning this to Felicieu, his reply gave life to a vague notion she'd carried since first meeting the dark stranger.

"I fly to Madagascar tomorrow. Why don't you stop there on your way to Kenya? You would be my guests."

Saying this, he put a hand on my arm, "I could show you some fascinating sights." He continued whetting our excitement by describing a Land Rover trek over mountains to isolated villages, and into national parks, home to lemurs and exotic birds.

His eyes flashed more brightly. "*Four J's*! Come and visit! My relatives would welcome you with a grand feast."

Was it fate meeting Felicieu? Should we stop at Madagascar under military rule; its borders closed as they had been for years. Mentioning this to Felicieu, he replied his family was influential and could help gain legal entry.

A great adventure beckoned, but should we chance it? Tapping my wife's finger, she turned with fire in her eyes. So I nodded, "Yes. We'll stop if we can."

Departing Mauritius ~

Caressing breezes took the good ship *Banyandah* across a quiet emptiness, blue on blue during the day, gliding under starry heavens each night. On the fifth day, our noon position showed Diego Suarez within two hundred miles, meaning two more nights at the same leisurely pace would see us off its coast just after daybreak, and that would be perfect. We'd have good light to reconnoitre the island before committing our ship to the unknown.

But fate had other plans. Dawn the next day saw the wind pick up. Stronger since midnight, now *Banyandah* no longer glides smoothly through the sea, she is racing the white marching army. We reduce sail, but the miles still scream past. If *Banyandah* keeps flying like this, we'll arrive too early, in darkness, and that would be dangerous.

Entering anywhere strange in the dark is courting danger. Sometimes the *Four J's* will try, sometimes not, depends on conditions. If discernible leading lights mark the route in and the weather permits, we might give it go. If there are winking red and green channel markers, that's much better. And if *Banyandah* has a detailed chart and pilot book describing the entry, it's usually a breeze. But not always is the sea kind nor every port well lit and we do not carry every chart. When the odds are against, attempting an entry comes down to good judgement, a stout boat, and a heap of courage. Success leads to strange, exciting places. Failure might not just injure pride, it risks death and destruction.

In the dawn's soft light, the sky looked harmless and unmoving, but the sea marched in high swells with their tops blown white. Overhead, the muted howl grew in strength, encouraging me to consider trying to reach Diego Suarez before night. If we don't, and the wind continues to build, we might not be able to drop sail and wait for the new morning's light. It might force us to run and lose our chance to visit Madagascar.

The Dead Don't Cry

No land is visible. After checking the miles on the log, I slip aft, careful not to wake Jude who's snug in her bunk after her watch. Leaning over the chart, I plot a dead reckoned position based on the course steered and miles travelled since our last known fix. After measuring the distance to Diego Suarez and checking my watch, I realise entering in daylight will be tight. One decisive factor is the current. According to the chart, it should be going north with us. If it is, and we push *Banyandah* to her limits, then we might reach port by last light.

Making the decision, I rush topsides to hoist the big sails, and *Banyandah* surges forward. The race is on. Navigation is now critical. Our landfall has to be perfect. Every wayward mile means extra time.

Storm or calm, racing or quiet at anchor, everyday life carries on. After the boys wake and breakfast is over, school begins. Jerome scribbles several pages of science notes while Jason works through an English lesson. Mid-morning arrives, Jude wakes and is straightaway handed a coffee by her little white mop, and she purrs in his cuddle. But when our eyes connect, she looks worried, so I blow her a kiss. Then after telling everyone about the deteriorating weather and the race, to calm their concern, I say we'll hove to if it doesn't work out. The boys get excited, but the worry lingers for Jude. She knows her man. She knows I learn mostly by trial and error.

The hours and miles continue to scream past. Every few minutes, one of us is jumping to the deck to scan the horizon, but so far, a disheartening task. Where is land? Will we make port by night?

At last, late in the day, although a mere thickening of haze along the horizon, it's land.

"Land Ho! Madagascar!" The cry flies aloft, lost to wind and sea. But it's the call all have awaited.

"Where?" Jerome asks, his hair flying as if poked out a speeding car.

"Are you blind or something?" retorts Jason. "Don't you see that grey stuff to the west?"

Less jubilant, a pensive thought clouding her face, Jude turns to me, her eyes asking, will we find safety before dark?

Only three hours of good light remain, and *Banyandah* is racing before a near gale still building. Her windvane working as if Hercules keeps our ship tracking straight upon the rising sea, obliquely closing with the east coast of Madagascar. If we could confirm our position, we would know exactly how far away lay Diego Suarez. But scanning the blur on the horizon, the only feature shown on our chart is a thousand-foot high mountain still obscured by haze.

Fate might decide this one. When setting out from Australia, Madagascar had not been on our route, and the only chart we have shows just a third of the island and another four-hundred miles of ocean to its north. Madagascar is the world's fourth-largest island, yet we see the two hundred fifty miles covered on our chart in an area no larger than two hand spans. At our current fast speed, an hour's sailing is less than a finger's thickness. Our destination, the ten-mile wide bay of Diego Suarez, is the size of a thumbprint, and its unknown entry is the width of a fat line. Before it are no headlands or bays offering shelter, no off-lying islands to shelter behind. The coast is straight with just a narrow band of reef in places. That means *Banyandah* can go in close to hopefully identify something.

On the chart, the island wears a dunce's cap at the northern end which comes to a point at Cap d'Ambre, where there's a lighthouse. Fifteen miles before that lighthouse is our destination, perhaps a half-mile break in the land opening due west, with another lighthouse on the southern side of this gap. On the chart, this lighthouse is marked by a magenta stroke printed right across the opening, making details even more challenging to find. Hidden under this magenta stroke could be tiny dots indicating a reef, or small crosses meaning rocks in the channel.

Land heights are not shown either, which means the opening could be a gash between two towering cliffs or lost in the darkness between two low-lying sand spits. But the chart shows the southern approach clean, and that means *Banyandah* can continue in close until the first lighthouse. Then a decision will have to be made.

Shadows lengthened and fade into night, and although now dark, *Banyandah* is close upon the coast running fast with twin headsails wing and wing and the mainsail still flying. Ahead, the lighthouse on the southern headland blinks. It would be foolhardy to try entering in such windy dark conditions, but everything seems under control, so my adventurous spirit prays for a sign indicating we should try, and suddenly I'm amazed by what might be that sign.

"Look! A ship! Hey, a ship's coming out!" I call below before racing forward for a better view.

The Dead Don't Cry

The headland must be tall cliffs because in the scant moonlight the ship's lights emerged from a black void.

Caught in one of those unstoppable moments, I'm leaping back and forth between deck and chart, hoping each time to discover a new detail. Jude is attempting to get the evening meal underway, but she's a yo-yo, jumping up and down the companionway not wanting to miss any of the action between carving up a fish landed earlier.

When abeam the gap, its impenetrable darkness gives no clues. Are there reefs in the channel? Why aren't there more navigation lights? Seconds pass while my heart thunders.

Oh, God, what should I do? For one final look, I dive into the chartroom. But damn! That tiny thumbprint is still the same. Back on deck, a sudden blaze of lights confronts me through the black gap.

"City lights!" I shout. "This place is huge!"

Still struggling to turn in or not, I turn forward to clear my thoughts and freeze. Seen only in my most frightening nightmares, the sails of my ship are silhouetted against an expanse of white lost to the dark unknown. In the dim moonlight it's a field of dirty snow, except there are distinct furrows. Unsure, or maybe unwilling to believe, a few heartbeats pass, then I'm screaming, "REEF!"

Oh, dear God. In my anxiety over whether to enter the bay of Diego Suarez, I had misjudged the distance of a few dots and dashes extending from the northern headland that must be a reef enclosing a lagoon. And *Banyandah* with her sails spread like the wings of a dragon is flying before an uncaring force towards a storm-battered coral edge.

Suddenly the noise of storm winds are silenced, there's nothing except an animal shrieking. "JUDITH! THE ENGINE FULL POWER!"

Running fast and screaming again, with every scrap of strength I rip loose the halyards holding the two forward sails.

Jude, below, trying to control her sudden panic, grabs her children and two life jackets and shouts, "Put them on." She'd heard the fear in her man. Next instant she's swept the night's dinner into the sink and running for the controls.

It's an old engine, but by God, she always fires first piston up. This time her roar sounds weak in the mayhem, but through the deck, Jude feels its reassuring rumble.

The sails are falling and Jude can see whitewater ahead, but can't hear me yelling, "RIGHT! TURN HARD RIGHT!" She only sees my arm jabbing wide to the right against dirty surf.

After all those miles and dramas, Jude's shoulders square up turning the boat while she checks the depth sounder then she's screaming, "We've only got six feet!"

Into the darkness, a white mop pokes up the cabin hatch and her youngest asks, "Mum, are we going to sink?" And a roar answers the child with spray whipped off the first breaker.

"Get below!" She commands, and pleads, "Whatever happens, stay put, and keep the hatch down."

Here's where luck first enters this disaster. With just a mainsail up, the storm winds helped our rudder slew *Banyandah* side-on to the breakers. And with full engine revs chewing a frothy sea, *Banyandah* hangs in space, not moving until the next comber comes out the night. So tall Jude's looking up, alarmed at its boiling white top shooting green sparks of bioluminescence. Hissing like a giant snake, it strikes taking Jude under, her hands desperately clinging to the wheel as whirlpools try to suck her away. Tons of ocean submerge *Banyandah's* foredeck forcing me underwater, hands locked around stays, fearing powerful forces will wash me away.

"This is it," came to me in full clarity. "The crunch of reef will be next. And then we'll be rolled over."

Surfacing after what felt minutes, an ocean of water is cascading off the decks. In the cockpit, Jude's gasping and sucking in wet air. Hearing her boys terrified screams above the mayhem, she's tortured, knowing she must guide the ship. But where? How? Panic wants control, and she shrieks, "Jack! Jack!"

Heedless of my need to be on deck, I rushed aft to reassure Jude, and a sword pierces my heart when I lift the hatch to see Jason consoling his sobbing brother, both in life jackets so bulky both seem no larger than babies.

I'm silently praying, "Oh, please God, don't let us hit the reef," just as Jude shouts, "Jack! We're not moving!"

The fear in her voice brings me back, and I yell, "We are moving! Just keep us pointing east! And keep cool, we'll make it."

The Dead Don't Cry

Wanting so much to give Jude's arm a reassuring squeeze, a new breaker came out the black night. Its only warning, a roar then a sickening thud of seawater flooding over our dodger, submerging the decks, filling the cockpit.

In waist-deep seawater, Jude's eyes stay fixed to the red glow of the compass in her fight to regain control. Our ship, leaden by the sheer weight of so much water, wallowed sluggishly before careening over to port. In a rush, tonnes of water spilt off *Banyandah*.

Hanging onto the dodger awaiting the next comber, I prayed our old engine didn't quit.

"C'mon Jude… Get us back to the east," I urged. "I'm going forward to raise sail."

Struggling forward braced against the railing to guide me through the blackness and hellish noise, I push against storm gusts. Roaring at full tilt, the engine battled us back towards open sea just as another comber hit. One blink, there's only darkness. The next, a wall glowing with green sparks washed me off my feet, and again life hangs in my grip of the rigging.

Pulling myself up, experience pays dividends. In Stygian blackness, all hell breaking loose, I raised one headsail by instinct and feel alone.

For what seemed a lifetime of fright, trapped in that hellish confusion where every roar of a wave, every jolt, every bump, sent fear shuddering through us wondering were there more reefs? Were we being driven back? In that blackness, how would we know?

We could only hold on tight, keep our course, and pray. Rigid and hardly breathing, not wanting to break the charm that's keeping our engine roaring and the sounder showing an increasing depth, we ever so slowly power-sailed more than a mile out to sea.

Only when far away from that reef would Judith let me turn north for the lighthouse atop Cape d'Ambre.

Three hours later, the boys in their bunks fast asleep in their life jackets, Jude turned *Banyandah* in the shore's direction with the engine beating rhythmically. We'd rounded Cap d'Ambre and were on the north side of the island, with the wind pushing us away from land and the sea far more peaceful.

In blackness that hides a man's hand in front of his face, a persistent quiver racked my body as we crept in using the sounder to find anchoring depth. When showing seventy feet, we dared go no closer and let go the anchor followed by heaps of chain. By touch alone, I found my way back to the welcome security of *Banyandah's* cockpit.

The engine secured, lights extinguished, suddenly our world became eerie. I found Jude curled in the corner by the helm. Pulling away from my touch, she wanted to be left alone in the darkness, so I stretched out on the other seat.

With the danger over, her rejection started me trembling. And no matter how strongly I willed it, I couldn't stop shaking. Lying back, my head taking the support of the seat, a breath held since that first comber hit escaped me. Crazy, but in its sigh, I heard the terrified cries of my children. Tears poured forth, and thoughts raced… *I live for the beauty and thrills my skills bring me…* I was to blame. Guilt engulfed me. More tears fell.

Forever a different man, I realised, but for a stroke of luck, God's will, whatever you wish to call it, we would have either been dead or feeling our ship being destroyed by a cruel sea. And if they weren't already dead, I might have been hearing the screams of my loved ones.

And why? Because of my mistake. The burden too great to bear, I turned to the privacy of the dark sea and wept.

Jude heard my sobs and came to draw me into her arms. She knows I'm more impetuous than a fool and had refused to commit our ship to the unknown. Stroking my ear, brushing curls from my neck, blowing cooling air onto my tears, hers joined mine falling freely as she whispered. "Love; we are one. You're my true north. I'll follow you to eternity." Then giving me an affectionate squeeze, "But hey, let's not go on that big adventure just yet."

MAYBE THE WORLD IS GROWING SMALLER

I'm guessing, but I'd say more than a million separate incidents had to fall just right for this chance meeting to happen as it did. Sure, the *Four J's* travel a lot and our chances of bumping into one particular person are probably better than many. But such an unusual encounter has to be classed an event.

Maybe not exactly a million incidents. Maybe more, maybe less, but one thing's certain. Our flash decision to board a bus and cross all of Turkey in one night was definitely a factor. From there, the events fell into place, one after another.

Timing... Does it matter? A second dallied here, a minute waiting for the change of a traffic light might change destiny. But the *Four J's* followed no timetable nor did we have a plan. In Istanbul, it took three days of non-stop touring, starting early each morning with breakfast among the sea of humanity filling the streets. Followed by mile upon mile of walking from one fascinating site to another. Exhausting days, found us waking early the fourth morning thinking any more sightseeing might ruin our special feeling for the city. So, giving no thought to where we'd end up that day, we sleepily trundled down the staircase lugging our packed kit bags in hand.

Without a guide or directions, we dragged our feet along empty streets to the waterfront. Soon the fresh air coming off the Bosporus popped open our eyes and seeing Asia looking back from the opposite shore we wondered how many land and sea battles had been commanded from where we stood. Placards told of centuries-old events, and our excitement soared recounting schoolbook stories of Caesar and Alexander the Great.

Further along the waterway, a ferry terminal appeared with notice boards listing timetables and destinations. It's so bewildering to see something familiar but unreadable. That prompted the *Four J's* to seek help from others strolling past. One, with gesticulating hands, in broken

English solved the mystery by explaining that some ferries sail thirty miles along the coast.

Taking one would offer unobstructed views of the ornate mosques and towering minarets as we departed Istanbul, cutting hours of bus travel through crowded suburbs. A check of the timetable showed that if we were quick, we could squeeze in a visit to the Ottoman Sultans last palace.

Timing... Again begs the question. Is timing essential with chance? In our case we missed the ferry we'd planned to take when our quick visit to the opulent *Dolmabahce Palace* didn't get squeezed in, our visit got stretched out. Where else would we find such fabulous jewels on display?

Instead, we caught a later ferry—one packed with holidaymakers and families with little ones chasing each other around the decks. Drifting on the wind, laughter mingled with the cries of babies. But the hubbub didn't spoil our day. On the move again and afloat made us feel right at home.

Mid-voyage I left the boat deck to check on my sons who earlier had wandered off to find a quiet spot to work on their scrapbooks. Going through a labyrinth of passageways, a gathering of Turks stopped me dead because I could hear my eldest son speaking from its centre.

"Yeah, we live on a boat," said Jason. "It's moored in Bodrum right now. We sailed all the way from Australia."

Jerome's voice cut in, "And we've been living onboard twelve years. Since I was two."

This created quite a buzz amongst the crowd as a few translated what the boys said while others exchanged comments in Turkish.

Then a woman spoke slowly, having difficulty with the English; "And you go to school or no?" The group hushed for the answer.

"Sure, we go to school," Jason replied. "Mum's our teacher. We have correspondence lessons from Australia."

Not wanting to be left out, Jerome quickly added, "And it's great. We learn heaps. Right now I'm studying Greek history and do you know what? We were just there."

Turning to walk back upstairs, I heard a man ask, "Can we look inside your scrapbooks? I would love to see something of the world like you do."

An hour later, a strip of yellow sand came up on the horizon backed by a clutter of small square white buildings and a single minaret marking Yalova, once the favourite holiday spot of the late, much loved Turkish leader Mustafa Kemal Ataturk.

With packs slung on our backs, we strolled off the gangplank and straight into a crowd of holiday-makers, getting a few curious glances. Well, we'd arrived. Now, what to do?

As if reading our mind, five youths ran up to us, bubbling with chatter. One called out, "Sprechen sie Deutsch? Speak English?"

That's when our gathering drew everyone's attention, especially as this happened right in the middle of the town's only roundabout with a statue of the great *Ataturk* himself staring down. Under a barrage of questions, somehow we moved the band off the street where I made a plea for help in finding cheap accommodation.

Here timing comes into it again. If we hadn't on a whim journeyed to Istanbul and missed the first ferry, and if we hadn't been stopped by those boys who so quickly found us lodgings - So many if's.

The countdown must have been ticking off the last few seconds after leaving our lodgings to stroll along the promenade with hundreds of Turkish holiday-makers. And must have nearly finished counting as we stopped at a bazaar to browse local trinkets. The last seconds ticked off when we stopped to buy ice cream from the man who had the stickiest ice cream we'd ever seen. Without knowing, zero struck when a boy our sons' age came up and softly asked, "Sprechen sie Deutsch?"

"Nah, we're from Australia, mate," joshed Jerome grinning mischievously.

"Really!" burst out from the teenager. "So am I!"

Just like in the movies. Our four heads snapped to look at this young man now beaming a broad smile.

"But, you're Turkish!"

"Yeah, but I grew up in Australia. I came here with my parents three years ago. We're going back later this year." His voice no longer sounded Turkish but came definitely from the land of Aus.

Each could feel something special taking place, and big smiles featured on everyone's faces as we exchanged more bits of information. Then Jude posed the question. "How do you like Turkish school?"

"Well, I don't exactly go to a Turkish school," he replied. "You see, learning the language was really hard when we first arrived. And Dad knew I'd be finishing my schooling in Australia, so I've been doing correspondence lessons here."

Anticipation quickly coloured Judith's face as she gasped. "Whose lessons do you use?"

"Well, we used to live near Brisbane, so I'm doing the Queensland lessons. What about you?"

Hearing this, the kids screeched. "You do Queensland correspondence? So do we!".

"No kidding! Hey, you're not the family sailing around the world, are you? And not waiting for an answer he added, "Was that your computer printed map in the yearbook?"

Jerome's pride burst forth. "Yeah, that's us. What grade are you in?"

"Grade ten."

"Oh wow, that's my grade," chirped Jason. "Who's your English teacher?"

Imagine what the ice cream seller must have thought, observing these five excited people chatting back and forth in a foreign tongue. When his curiosity could take no more, he sang out something that must have meant, *What's up?* And our new friend responded in rather impressive Turkish, and while their conversation ebbed back and forth,

Maybe the World is Growing Smaller

so did the *Four J's*. The amused shakes of the vendor's head matched ours in a moment when life astonished us all.

After a final burst of Turkish, the ice cream seller popped an even bigger grin on his face and began thrusting cone after cone upon us.

"He thinks it's magic," the lad replied to our curious looks. "He thinks it's a sign of good luck. The ice creams are his present."

"Hmm, this is great," Jude got out between licks of the most unusual goo she'd ever tasted. Then suddenly I asked, "Hey! What's your name?"

"My name is Kemal, like the great Turkish leader."

Kemal—a boy like our sons and like the many other sons being taught by the same school, sharing the same teachers. Only this school isn't the one down the street. This school serves young people all over Australia and scattered throughout the world. And from its few students scattered amongst the millions of people around the world, the *Four J's* just bumped into one of them in a little resort town on the Aegean Coast of Turkey. Amazing! Maybe the world is growing smaller!

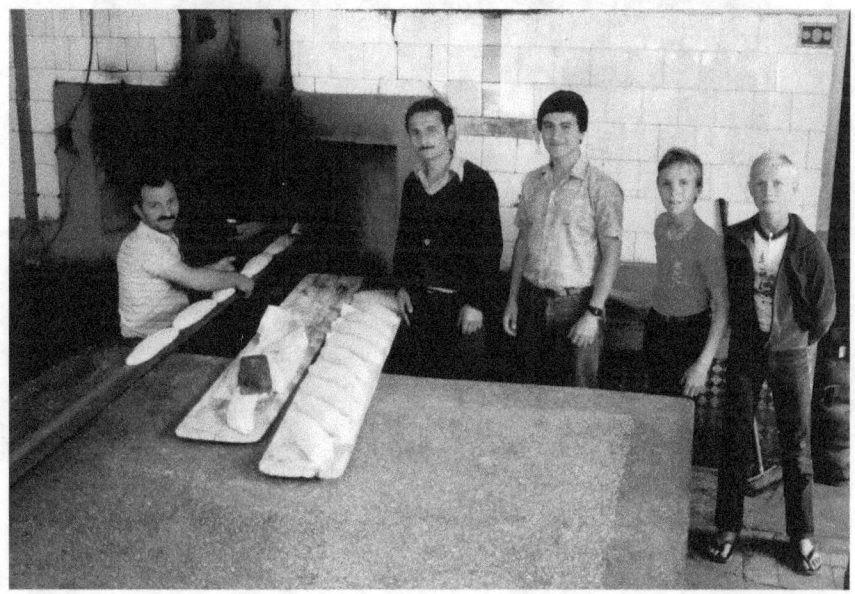

Kemal with his father and chief baker

Reflections in a Sailor's Eyes

Jason's Journal: Saturday 22 June 1985

A cold shower in the morning woke me up. When we were walking to the meeting place, we met Kemal on the road. Before we did anything, we asked him where he gets his hair cut. It cost 3.50 Turkish Lira each for a haircut. Then after a cup of chai (tea), we had breakfast. Next, we walked to his flat. Dad and Mum talked to his parents, and I played mastermind with him. They invited us to lunch. We had rice, aubergine (eggplant), chips, salad and cherries. Then as Dad had to do something in Yalova, Jerome and I split. Tomorrow we head back to Bodrum.

Jerome's Journal: Saturday 22 June 1985

Met him on the street and asked him to take us to his barber. So he did, and we got a haircut. I look handsome now. He took us to his house, and we had lunch there. Watched a film on Turkey then loafed the whole afternoon away. Got back to the hotel at 7 pm walked around town looking for a pizza parlour.

Ephesus Turkey

MALPELO LESSONS

The day began like many others aboard the good ship *Banyandah*. At first light our anchorage was found to be encased in a wispy mist that softened the morning's warmth and light, making sounds far-away whispers. There in the timeless stillness our floating home lay so quietly at rest she felt afloat in space instead of on the calm waters off Colon at the entrance to the busy Panama Canal. On this third morning at its Atlantic entrance, we were still preparing *Banyandah* for her transit through the locks to the Pacific Ocean scheduled for three days time.

Upon rising that morning came a feeling of isolation like being adrift. There was no haste, no need to rush. It seemed a perfect day for study, a day to ponder our future.

After breakfast, the boys were set to work on their school lessons. Around our main table they spread their books and papers and in a short time came silence, a scene straight from any classroom. Well, maybe not just any classroom. After all, they were aboard a yacht, parked in what was probably the most heavily trafficked canal in the world. Somewhere outside, away from us, tug boats were working, their occasional toots reminding us of their presence.

Jason, fifteen now, was lost to the present as soon as he opened his book. Looking over his shoulder, he was in South America with Simon Bolivar and his armies. While next to him, Jerome, a year younger struck a more thoughtful pose, head down, his shaggy white hair clasped between two little hands. He too was enmeshed in learning, away somewhere in the geological intricacies of the Pacific Ocean's tectonic plates.

Eventually the mist thinned and a stream of ships became visible, one following another, their superstructures disappearing into the jungle-clad land to begin their journey to the Pacific.

Settling in with the boys was Jude, always around, either herself studying or ready to assist. On this quiet day when everything was running smoothly, Jude was busy cleaning cupboards and sorting lockers, preparing for the next load of provisions.

And me? Well, after everyone had settled and a hush had fallen over the boat, I tucked myself into a peaceful spot in the stern cabin and pulled out our huge stack of world charts. We needed a plan, and that morning seemed the perfect time to find one.

What was needed was a route to follow after exiting the Panama Canal and back in the same ocean as Australia. We knew that once in the Pacific we'd be heading south for Ecuador. But by which route? So it was time to study the charts.

Our next destination was Guayaquil in the southern part of Ecuador. This had been decided many months earlier when off the West African coast in the Canary Islands. During a dinner party in *Banyandah's* spacious cockpit another yachting couple, who the year before had sailed South America's East Coast, told us many lively, amusing tales of their South American adventures under such a stunning star studded, moonless night, a night when dreams seem easily made into reality that we made the decision to visit that continent. We particularly wanted to visit Ecuador because they administered the Galapagos Islands whose unique wildlife so powerfully influenced Charles Darwin. We wanted to share what Charles Darwin had found so profound with our children. It was a difficult dream to achieve back then because obtaining permission to take a private vessel through that archipelago was almost impossible.

You won't succeed unless you try is an axiom that has opened many a closed door in our lives. So when still in the Canary Islands, we thought that if we went to Ecuador we could visit the naval authorities and personally plead our case. That clinched our decision. Ecuador, here we come!

We had no personal contacts in Ecuador, nor had we heard any reports from other yachtsmen. So we had little information other than what we'd gleaned from borrowed books on attractions like the Inca Trail or the animals of the upper Amazon. The information we had on wind and current showed we'd probably have a battle to windward down South America's west coast. It also looked like we'd be bucking a fairly hefty current which looked like it got stronger the further south we went. Both, the headwind and current indicated hard work winning miles.

Malpelo Lessons

In the positive our World Book did make Ecuador sound a stable place, which in South America was a definite plus especially since we needed a reliable mail drop for returning school work. At that time both Jason and Jerome were enrolled with the Queensland Correspondence School, which throughout our entire three year circumnavigation proved an excellent institution with good teachers and resources. So just before leaving the Canary Islands to cross the Atlantic, we opened our atlas to Ecuador and saw that Guayaquil was its major port. It had the necessary officials to clear in our ship and could be a first port of call, therefore General Delivery, Guayaquil became the return address for the schoolwork that was ready to be sent off.

Ten weeks later in Colon, with another five thousand miles under our keel and the Atlantic and Caribbean now recorded memories in our journals, I settled into the stillness of our stern cabin to decide our exact route south to Ecuador. Sitting on the floor in the comfy nook created by our U shaped bed, with maps of places yet to be visited and charts showing wind and current patterns spread across our bed. Studying the various routes, I took note of the Humbolt Current's cold northerly set and imagined the bays and ports upon the coast, the mountains we'd see from offshore.

Banyandah's aft cabin is a lovely place to dream of far away places. Like a mother's womb holding tranquil peace, that on such a quiet day was perfect for meditation. With eyes partly closed and my ship smooth and quiet under me, my fingers traced routes while I imagined the passage miles sliding past. For a time I was lost on this make believe voyage, lost in what soon might be real life.

It was after this thinking and dreaming, more or less by fate that our final route was decided. Only when my finger traced further out into the ocean did my eye catch sight of a very tiny dot. It was such a small dot, easily missed among the chart's other markings until I spotted the figures eight hundred and fifty in brackets next to it. Those figures made me reach for the pilot. After reading a bit, I excitedly picked up my dividers and measured the distance from Panama to the dot called Malpelo, then from Malpelo to Ecuador. Right then a light turned green in my head. I had my route. I had found a mid-ocean turning point. Better than that, we had the makings of an adventure. Grabbing the chart I rushed out of the cabin.

"Hey Kids! Guess what!" I blurted out breaking into their work as I stepped across the forward companionway waving the chart. "There's an enormous rock jutting out the ocean right on our route to South America."

Both boys stopped writing mid-sentence, their eyes fastening onto mine with such quickening interest that a grin instantly creased my face.

"It's called Malpelo, and it belongs to Colombia."

Jason's mouth dropped hearing this. He knew from our earlier talks that Colombia was dangerous. It's not that he was afraid. He just knew I did crazy things sometimes and so I went on, "Don't worry, guys, it's three hundred miles off their coast."

Jude hearing the excitement in my voice lifted her eyes from a teaching manual and locked them onto mine with that special glint I knew only came when she sensed an adventure in the making. I winked. "Just what you like, babe. Probably no one lives on it. It's just a rock taller than a skyscraper and it's all by itself in the middle of the ocean."

"Yippee. That's great!" Jerome gushed, jumping up on the settee and knocking his school work to the floor. "Let's go exploring!"

Seeing Jude's smile set my imagination on fire. "Yeah, we'll go exploring." I promised. "We'll climb all over it - if we can find a spot to anchor." I added this to calm down the kids. "That's the problem. The dot on our chart is surrounded by ocean marked thousands of feet deep."

Dancing eyes lit the two brothers' faces as they pushed each other, wrestling playfully. Pausing for a second, Jason beamed a confidence I didn't feel and gleefully announced, "Anchoring! No problem, dad." Then Jerome stopped laughing long enough to chime in, "You'll find a way, dad. You always do. C'mon, let's go there!"

It is lovely to be a child without responsibilities and not need to make decisions. The boys did some of the work, but it was I who commanded the ship and directed where it went. At times a difficult position. Especially when balancing adventure with safety which often demanded swift decisions when lives and ship were at risk. At that moment prudence seemed the best course. "No promises guys." I said getting up from my comfy spot on the companionway. "I'll check around the other boats for a more detailed chart. But just think lads. A mountain erupting out an empty ocean. You know what that means."

Sure they did.

Malpelo Lessons

"Adventure! Adventure!" they both sang and giggles followed me aft as I went to find more about Malpelo.

Malpelo Passage

Our passage from Panama to Malpelo drifted along on light breezes that came and went. Some hours we moved sweetly. At other times, we bobbed about like a bit of flotsam. But the miles always slipped past with never a worry, and that's when we enjoy being at sea in Nature's world, our hatches wide open and the sun streaming in.

Other than the quietness of the sea, the only other event being the passage of the sun overhead. No, not the everyday event that everyone sees. I mean the astrological event where the sun crosses the same latitude as the observer. What's latitude do I hear?

For a moment, imagine a basketball, next put lines from the North Pole to the South Pole. Those we call longitude, and they are the east/west component of our navigational grid. Now, the special line around the Earth's middle equidistance from both poles is the equator, and it's the zero line of latitude. Unlike longitude, lines of latitude encircle the Earth parallel to the equator and form the north/south component of our navigational grid.

Because the Earth is tilted, exactly where the sun strikes the Earth perpendicularly shifts north and south of the Equator as the year progresses. For example, on March 20, the sun shines directly onto the Equator, and all around the world, there is equal day and night called the equinox. By June 21, the sun is as far north as it is going, and shining directly onto the Tropic of Cancer at 23½ degrees north latitude. 'The longest day' Americans like to say. After that, the sun heads south until on September 23, the sun re-crosses the Equator, the zero latitude, when again day and night are equal. On and on the sun moves south until on December 22, it is shining directly on the Tropic of Capricorn at 23½ degrees south latitude. That's the farthest south the sun goes, and in Australia, it's champagne and prawns on the barbie. Then the sun drifts back over the Equator on March 20. That's part one of today's celestial navigation lesson.

Part two has to do with navigating when the sun goes from being south of the ship to being north, or vice versa. In either case, navigating gets tricky when the sun passes directly overhead as it did for us on April

5. Not because the sun's intense heat scrambled our brains, but because sextant-swinging navigators like the *Four J's* rely on measuring the angle between the sun and the horizon, that's the 'altitude.' And when this altitude is large, as it will be when the sun is directly overhead, the accurate measuring of that angle can be tricky.

Sextant navigation is a terrific way to stay in tune with the Earth's natural movements. A sextant is a handheld device with a small telescope that has adjustable shades and two mirrors, one of which is connected to an arm that can be rotated through an arc to track the sun's rise or fall in the heavens. Our sextant on *Banyandah*, the one used to navigate more than a hundred and fifty thousand miles, is a full-size bronze Tamaya that has been out in all kinds of weather, suffering a bit of neglect.

When looking through the telescope, the image is split in two. The left side sees straight through to whatever we're pointing the sextant at, which is usually the horizon. The right side reflects off the index mirror, which can be rotated to track stars, or the sun through adjustable shades. Through the scope, the sun or stars can be anything from a sharp, bright orb in a clear sky, to a fuzzy blob hardly distinguishable through cloud.

On this voyage, we saw a pencil straight horizon. But during storms, the horizon can be a turmoil of white water dropping out of view as the ship bobs up and down with passing waves. In those conditions, only the best skills and good luck get a good sight.

When measuring the altitude of the sun, the idea is to maintain the sun 'sitting' on the horizon by adjusting the angle of the index mirror. Somewhat complicating this is the speed at which the sun rises or falls, which changes during the day, being fastest at sunrise and sunset, and slowest as the sun approaches its highest altitude. When at its highest point, for some seconds the sun in the telescope doesn't move and no further adjustment is required. When the sun stops rising is celestial noon, and that's when the sun is precisely north or exactly south of your position, and it's easy to determine your latitude. But in those rare instances when the sun is dead overhead on the same latitude, it is trickier.

I began my navigation lesson in the main cabin our second morning out with my two star pupils alert, notebooks open and pens poised.

"You know boys the sun will pass directly overhead today. And right this minute the sun is marching straight at us dead out the east." I stepped across the narrow cabin and leant against the galley bench where I could gaze upon the passing sea.

"The sun will rise until reaching its zenith around noon when it'll pass just a smidgen off directly perpendicular. Now you've been tracking the sun these last few days, so you know its arc is becoming very flat. Today when you look, the sun's arc will be really flat. And if the sun passes directly overhead, meaning its rays pass through us to the exact centre of the earth then the arc will appear so flat in the sextant you'll be able to pivot around in a complete circle and see the sun lying smack on the horizon." And with that, I shaped my hand like a sextant and held it up to my eye like a modern-day Captain Cook tracking an imaginary sun.

"Okay, here are some pointers. The sun will not be moving slowly as when further north or south of us. At its highest point, it'll click from rising to falling in an instant. So you've got to be ready. You've got to know which side the sun will pass. I mean, whether the sun passes north or south of us. That's important so you can point the sextant in that direction. If you point it the wrong direction, you will get readings over ninety degrees, and that won't be any flipping good."

Catching my breath, I looked for signs of doubt or confusion. But both boys still looked eager and comfortable in the crooks of the settee, so I continued. "Jerome, you're navigator today. Will the sun still be passing south of us, or to our north?"

"Still in the south," he replied quick as a wink.

"How do you know?"

A moment's hesitation filled his blue eyes. He knew he'd been right, but how to explain. He wanted to be exact because he knew I'm a demanding teacher, one not afraid to badger his students. And

why shouldn't I? They need to understand the material under pressure because a heaving deck in a storm can be a mighty lonesome place, where a bit of knowledge stiffens the backbone.

Jerome glanced through his notes then his head popped up. "Ah, the sun's declination at noon will be six degrees north latitude. We're not quite that far south yet, so the sun will still pass south of us."

"Good son, I agree." And I reached over and gave his hair a ruffle. "The sun is moving further north at the rate of point nine of a mile each hour. You'll find that number at the bottom of the daily pages in the nautical almanac. Next to the little 'd', which stands for hourly differences."

Both heads sank to the blue soft covered book open before them.

"That's the sun's change in latitude each hour," I explained. "Look ahead and you'll see that the rate changes during the year. Fastest when the sun crosses the equator, slowest when it changes direction at the Tropic of Cancer and Tropic of Capricorn. At those outward points, the sun's movement is so slow it stays at that extreme declination for almost a day."

Pages were ruffled, fingers pointed, heads nodded.

"Makes sense. Can't have the sun rebounding with a bang at the end of each cycle. A sine wave, I think." And my hand swished through the air in the familiar figure of eight pattern.

"See. Fastest when crossing the middle. Slowest when changing direction at the extremes."

One reward of teaching is seeing your pupils understand; it shows in their eyes as it did in my sons.

"You two are lucky." They didn't know why, but my comment prompted a bit of horseplay, which stopped when I continued. "There will be a large enough difference today to know which way to point your sextant, and with the sun going north and us going south, tomorrow there'll be enough difference to know to point the sextant in the other direction."

Outside, a sparse wind lightly disturbed the sea creating bright twinkling tops amongst the blue that kept us moving with hardly any movement in the ship. So much beauty had me feeling cooped up and I knew that I'd soon need to go topsides to search the far horizon, and if I felt energetic, I might even climb the mast for a long distant view around our blue world. But first I needed to finish the lesson.

Glancing over to Jude in the starboard jump seat watching me with a mischievous twinkle, she quizzed me, "Remember the first time we had the sun cross the latitude we were on? It happened on our very first ocean voyage."

The years rolled back until that monumental foul-up came to mind. As it did, Jude's infectious twinkle played upon my lips, and I turned to the boys, "Okay you two. Here's a story you'll enjoy." And immediately I reaped the joy of seeing their eyes brighten. They fussed settling themselves knowing next would come another instalment of early *Banyandah* life.

Taking a breath, I wondered where to begin. "Remember, I had no navigational training before we took off the first time. Your mother took lessons at night school, but I'd been so busy building the boat, I figured I'd learn as we travelled. So off we went, up Australian's east coast making navigational blunders left, right, and centre. Believe me, its fortunate Australia is so big because for five months all I need do was keep Australia on our left and not run into anything." Twitters of laughter came from the boys, and I could only toss up my hands and shake my head.

"In between making foul-up after foul-up, I would hole up in the stern cabin with your mum's navigation notes trying to make some sense of celestial navigation. My engineering training helped because as you're finding out, navigation is knowing angles and planes. At first, not much made sense. The only part I learned was the ancient mariner's first tool, the noon sight. For the rest, the longitude part, I found a form in a navigation book that I filled out using step-by-step instructions. I followed that form religiously because the numbers meant nothing to me.

"Around November that first year, we're at Lizard Island inside the Great Barrier Reef where now there's a resort, but back then there was nothing, the island was ours entirely. The trade winds howled as they had the entire way up the coast from Sydney and returning south as planned seemed too hard a task. Hiding behind Lizard, there seemed only one course, keep going north and make our first ocean crossing to Papua New Guinea."

Sucking in a breath, remembering how I'd felt started me shaking my head and being an emotional fellow, I even fought back a tear. In the jump seat, Judith gave her ponytail a shake then leant towards the kids. "I remember your Dad sitting in the cockpit with angry grey clouds whistling over the hills, rolling smoke after smoke. He rolled a whole pile in preparation for going to sea."

"Yuk!" Jason cut in, "Shouldn't smoke."

"Yeah. Well, those first years were pretty nerve-racking. Okay for you at two and three. You just waddled around nude and played on long sandy beaches."

Hearing this, their young faces broke into sheepish grins, and they began jostling each other again.

"Okay, guys. Settle down." Waiting till they did, "So we set sail on our first ocean passage, and surprisingly the journey proceeded smoothly. The weather wasn't as bad as along the coast, so crossing a sea seemed easier than along the coast because there wasn't anything to bump into.

"Each day, I did the sextant swinging bit and used the tables to work out a fix. I knew nothing but that form and followed it one square at a time. As I mentioned, everything went along real fine, until the last day. What hadn't registered was, as we sailed north the sun continued marching south. And although each day my altitude readings got bigger, approaching ninety-degrees, I gave that not one thought. Just point and shoot, that's all I knew."

One of the boys cried out, "Oh Dad, you're smarter than that."

"Not really, I was learning a whole new way of life." Holding up a hand, "Let me go on, there's a lesson in this."

"That last day, land was getting close. An unknown land, with offshore reefs and low-lying islands and I am nervous. My first navigation sights had plotted all over the place, miles from each other, and because we might reach land in the blackness of night, our last day's noon sight became paramount. Realising that, I went on deck several minutes early with a plan to track the sun well before its highest point. But boy! Did I ever get a shock. When I adjusted the sextant and took a look, the sun was already well over eighty-nine degrees, almost dead overhead. In the next minute, it recorded over ninety. I knew it's not supposed to do that! In a stew, my stomach set hard like concrete, and crossing an ocean on a small boat seemed insane because everywhere looked the same. I damn near panicked, but calmed myself by knowing I needed thinking power to find the reason. Not knowing exactly what happened, I pictured the triangle formed by the sun, boat, and horizon, and realised we must have passed under the sun. Hurriedly I pointed the sextant in the other direction to the south."

Here, my hands went up in despair. "Sighting the sun in that direction recorded a reading well below ninety. I was too late. The sun had passed its highest point and was already falling. I'd blown it. Our very first landfall coming that night and I didn't know where we were."

The kids started laughing, Jude joined them, and I could only stand there looking the idiot.

"It sounds funny now," I cut in, "but not so then. I was a raw beginner, knew nothing, and it shook me. Knowing what I know now, I could have done other things. Like taking star sights, a look at the moon, or just stopping the boat till we figured out where we were. But even stopping *Banyandah* in the middle of a sea I feared because we'd never done that before and only vaguely knew how to do it. So we sailed on."

Still chuckling, Jude told her sons, "Everything worked out. Although your dad and I got so scared, we stood on deck until spying the blink of a lighthouse just before dawn. But, during that awful time before seeing the light, our imaginations drove us crazy, making every sound the crash of breakers, and every white splash the death edge of a reef. The boat didn't become a wreck, but we sure did."

While the boys pondered the importance of spot-on navigation, I let them in on another secret. "Hey! Here's the punch line. That light flashed a different sequence from the one expected. Seems I also missed my landfall by over twenty miles."

"Twenty miles!" exploded Jason, jumping off the settee, "We've never been that far out."

"No," I said with a knowing smile, "That's because you've got a good teacher. So remember," I said, putting more steel in my voice, "today and tomorrow, before you go up on deck, know everything you can about your sight. Know which way to point the sextant, the exact time for the sun's zenith, and expect it to move fast." Motioning topside with my head, "Navigation class is over. Let's take a break."

Banyandah School

Malpelo Lessons

Landfall at Malpelo

On passage day three, when only a day away from Malpelo, the wind threw off its lethargic bubble of laziness and began to blow with some enthusiasm as if bored by us loping along so slowly. Hour by hour as we recorded bigger mileage, I took the good news below to give the family a revised landfall hour.

After sunset that final night, our voyage became everything we love about sailing an ocean; a calm sea, caressing breeze, an arrow straight passage under a black, infinite sky punctuated by billions of heavenly bodies.

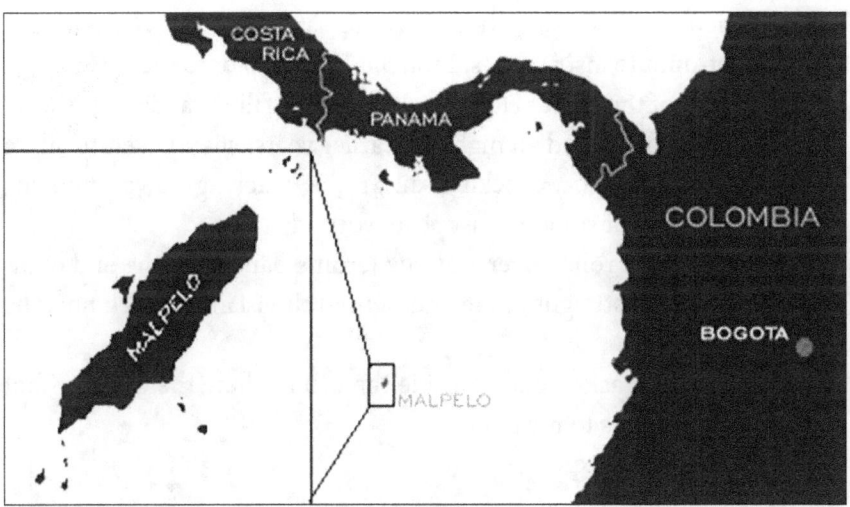

Long after Jude and the boys had gone to bed, with the boat hushed and quietly moving under its own guidance, I lazed back in the cockpit and looked up into that eternity of awesome majesty. My first reaction that of a beast confronted by something it doesn't understand, and my mind shied from questions posed by its unfathomable depth. Above the familiar shape of *Banyandah's* sails swaying darkly across the brilliance of our universe, *Pleiades*, the seven sisters, a rosette of twinkling stars like a pendant of diamonds, this night was lost in a collage of stars so vast I shook my head in disbelief then laughed aloud as I felt the creator enter my spirit.

Close to my ear I heard the soft gurgle of sea gypsies slipping past, and reassured by these old friends, the restraints on my mind slipped free. I soared up through particles of starlight hearing the strange sound of cetaceans communicating to one another. With my mind reaching for the heavens, these sounds became forests growing in the wind, producing images that flicked past until I began to relive moments not yet sorted. Wandering through my history, I revisited past judgements and sorted them not by right or wrong, but by intent, and through this cleansing process, I came to grips with my failings as a person.

At midnight, with only forty-five miles to go, I woke Jason for his two-hour watch. Judith watches two to four, after which Jerome watches till six. Under the immensity of our star-filled night, Jason and I sipped mugs of cocoa while he sleepily donned his safety harness. Giving him a kiss and last-minute instructions, I watched him clip onto the lifeline that ran the length of the deck before going below to fall immediately asleep. Quite a change from landfall nights of earlier years when I used to yo-yo between bunk and deck, checking sails, ropes, tracking down annoying rattles, or looking for ships, or just plain worried.

Upon waking, I rolled over and saw Jerome dancing at the end of his safety line looking straight at me and figured the island of rock must be in sight.

"What's up?" I asked once outside the cabin where the chill air shot rapid wake up signals to my brain.

"I had a fish!" he exploded.

"When?"

"He struck just as I was putting the line over the side. A huge one. I almost lost the whole rig!"

I smiled at the thought of Jerome, his white hair dancing in the crisp morning breeze, probably gazing about his private world of Nature while paying lure and line over the side. When WHAM! Jolted and shocked, a moment of panic, the fishing rig almost jerked from his grip.

"I had to grab a stay, or I'd have lost the lot," he sped on, his blue eyes darker in the morning light, wide with that special excitement known to youth.

"So where's this monster?" I asked with a teasing lilt in my voice.

"Oh, he got away. Probably the best thing, Dad. He was enormous. A monster!"

Malpelo Lessons

"Uh-huh." My smile spread into a grin as I pulled Jerome into my arms for a loving cuddle, his head nesting perfectly in the crook of my neck. The world ours, father and son, surrounded by blue beauty and freedom of life. That moment could have gone on forever.

"Seen any land?" I spoke into his hair, tasting salty freshness.

"Nah. Nothing yet. But some birds have been about."

"Oh?" I broke our embrace. "Where? When?"

Jerome backed away a pace, his lithe wiry frame showing young bulging muscles when he gripped the stainless rail while scanning the northern horizon.

"There!" He pointed just aft of *Banyandah's* beam, and following his lead, I saw at least three boobies swooping and diving into the sea.

Called gannets in some parts of the world, boobies are big birds the size of an eagle with long, pointed bills shaped precisely like the nose of a Concorde jet. Regarded as one of the best diving seabirds, their only compromise to perfect sleekness are two enormous pop-up eyes, a distinctive yellow against their white plumage and yellow beak, with feet of various colours; pink, blue, grey depending on species. These three took turns diving into a school of small fish. High into position they'd fly. Then wings at reverse pitch, they'd halt, fold their wings back to form a missile diving arrow straight into the sea and bob up seconds later with a fish. Boobies inhabit most islands in the tropical belt, with large colonies on the isolated ones. They're not migratory, nor lovers of long-distance flying, so they are a sign to sailors that land is near. The more birds - the closer the land.

A sharp call similar to a cockatoo swung our attention towards *Banyandah's* masthead.

"Hey! A Tropic Bird," I cried when I saw its white plumage and extraordinarily long tail feathers. "Amazing son. It looks so delicate and yet lives one of the toughest lives."

And as if agreeing, we heard again, "Swak! Swak!" This time just above our heads.

Jerome and I, our naked sides touching, leant against the rail watching this single visitor hover with fast-beating wings as it inspected the intruders into its world. One last call, dipping a wing Mr Bosun then soared away followed by two extraordinarily long tail feathers.

"Land's got to be near, son. The birds are coming out to greet us."

Dead ahead I saw sea ruffled by an occasional touch of white, backed by a smooth horizon and light blue sky with a stirring of milk. Just a titch to our right, a solid lump of white stood out. Clouds on the horizon always tweak my mind and scanning this one more closely I saw what my subconscious suspected.

"Jerome, see that cloud just right of the bow?" When he found what I meant, "See anything odd?"

"Hey, that's land!" He cried as recognition hit. "It's sharp and straight on its left. The rest is changing shape."

"That's right! Remember, when land's near, especially high land, look closely at the clouds." I gave him a playful push. "Well, you're on watch, go record our landfall in the log."

Malpelo, a solitary monolith hiding in a vast expanse of ocean, and yet my students made another perfect landfall.

An hour later, clear of cloud, Malpelo appeared a massive bleached bone-white column challenging the isolation of its ocean world. Rising vertically out the sea, that monolith soared free of vegetation, capped by a roundish baldhead. Close off its northern tip, three spires of jagged rock jutted out the sea. Otherwise, its world vacant, a lone sentinel watching over the seas.

Malpelo Lessons

Jason came up next, awakened by Jerome's nudge and his whispering, "Malpelo's in sight."

Dozy with sleep, he climbed into the cockpit clutching a tee shirt close to his chest and looked about before leaving the protection of the wheelhouse to join us standing on the stern deck. The morning breeze tousled his hair and popped open his eyes.

"Wow! It's stark!" His first words, followed by, "Sure one huge rock."

Naturally, with such a curious monster dominating our world, we three got excited and began talking loudly.

Jason retrieved our binoculars, and after examining Malpelo, suggested, "Hey, let's climb to the top."

Jerome screwed up his face, "Oh Jas, first we have to see if we can anchor. Can I have the glasses now?" He added with a touch of childishness.

Jason wasn't paying any attention. Instead, he'd panned the binoculars slowly across the sea and up into the sky. "Look!" he shouted, pointing astern. "Here comes a flock of boobies like a squadron of fighter planes."

"They're going to attack the lure," I warned Jerome, who'd given up waiting for the glasses and sat next to the trolling line on the life raft.

"Quick, Jerome!" Jas yelled. "They're diving! Pull the line in! Pull it!"

Zoom, splash, two at a time, boobies dove like Kamikaze pilots, and only Jerome's fast action, yanking the trolling line just as they splashed, made them miss the lure's deadly hooks. We've had birds suicide before.

"Look at that one," Jerome called after one of them surfaced and looked around bewildered. Matching the bird's antics, he pitched his voice low and lisped, "Ah, where'd it go?"

What an incredible sight, *Banyandah* under sail—a floating magic carpet going through blue space with the three of us laughing and pointing at those crazy birds dive-bombing our lure.

"Hey you lot. What's going on back there?" Jude's sharp voice snapped us about. Standing in the cockpit, naked except for panties, a hand up shielding sleep sensitive eyes, one side is creased from her night's rest.

"Mum! The island's in sight. Look! It's splendid!"

She turned and gazed ahead. A slash of sunlight slanting through the sails flashed back and forth across her bare back. A moment passed then she moved from the wheelhouse to the foredeck still staring forward at Malpelo. We three remained aft, happy just to watch her against the backdrop of the barren white rock, until finally, her head inched back and forth. Turning half around, an elfin smile lit her face. In years of travelling, Jude has seen many sights. Some like this have been powerful encounters provoking profound reactions. Jude's face displayed peaceful wonder knowing only Nature can create such a marvellous masterpiece. For a moment, that glow remained on her face while the three of us shared the same thought. Then she shrugged as if awakening from a dream.

"Another hour?" she asked.

I wagged my finger playfully, "More like two. It's bigger, and further than it looks."

"Ah, good," and turning she gave Malpelo a couple more slow nods as if acknowledging its might before turning back to me. "I'm going to make some coffee. Want some?"

Her eyes caught the boys, their dazzle hardening. "If we still have a couple of hours, you have time for a bit of school. Jerome, you should do maths. Jason, you can use the big table and finish your English essay." Abruptly like a Sergeant Major getting on with the day, she turned below, leaving us three high sea adventurers shaking our heads and swallowing giggles.

The Rock

Two hours later, seabirds filled the air, wheeling above in tight circles, their tail feathers flashing open and shut as they applied brakes to avoid collisions. It seemed they all wanted the closest view of the neighbourhood's newest sea creature. Next to *Banyandah,* and less than the proverbial stone throw, stood the rock face of Malpelo. In the calm conditions, out of daredevil delight I had brought us close until every fissure, every fragment of stone could be examined as if within reach of our hands. Now, Malpelo so high, our hearts beat an exciting tattoo in our upturned throats. While around our ship and right up to this giant, a Prussian blue world plummeted into immeasurable depth. With Jude guiding the helm, the boys and I kept watch at the bow as our ship slipped between this towering creature and the three jagged spires just off it.

"Keep your eyes peeled for discoloured water," I warned the boys. "Like that patch over there," I added after sighting a lighter area warning of an underwater obstruction close to our right.

Having handed the jib, only our mainsail remained filled with a comfortable breeze that propelled us through this Disneyland of wondrous sights. Accompanied by a chorus of birds, on our left erupted a vertical grey rock curtain that stretched from ocean to Malpelo's lofty peak. Red-brown streaks, darkening toward their edges and outlined in black, flowed down as if old blood from a wound in our sentinel's side. Coming off this curtain, a ridge of spiked stones ran from our giant's shoulder like an arm pointing to the sea. Where the sentinel's hand should have been, the arm ended in a cascade of rubble.

Ghosting along, *Banyandah* passed this crumbled hand close enough to see insects hopping up and down, doing their dance to the wash of the sea. Here stood a world untouched by time, and us its first explorers. Accompanied by the frantic cries of seabirds swarming overhead, we edged past the crumbled hand to enter a slight cove hardly more than a dent in our sentinel's side. Its opposite shore faced east to greet a new day's sun, making it appear as if our giant knelt out of great depths.

Scanning the slopes, what looked like a polka dot mantle spread across what I took to be his back, and the thousands of white dots on the grey rock blurred into a coronation robe over a sovereign's shoulders. In blinding light, we saw more fantasy. The robe moved! Tiny vibration like movements gave it life. Through the glasses those animated dots changed to thousands upon thousands of white-breasted seabirds guarding nests. Following our sentinel's back, more birds defended patches of open ground. Continuing down the curve of Malpelo's spine, we tracked increasing life until the glasses found solid blue.

Dropping my hands, I gazed up to the sky to let its softness quell the rising beat of my heart. Tracking Malpelo from sea to peak several times, the wonder grew within me. Hardly a mile long, a mountain erupting from the sea, nothing green, nothing in fact but the harshness of Nature and creatures strong enough to survive.

"Jack! Where do you want me to steer?"

Jude's call from the helm snapped me back to the moment, back as husband and father, to being an explorer surrounded by danger. Wiping a hand across my cheeks I looked about with the eyes of a sailor. "Start the engine," I ordered hoarsely, trying to settle my breath. "Then turn up into the wind. We'll take in sail before checking out that bay." Smoothly, without a bother, we did our work transforming *Banyandah* from a voyager of oceans to an explorer of tiny bays.

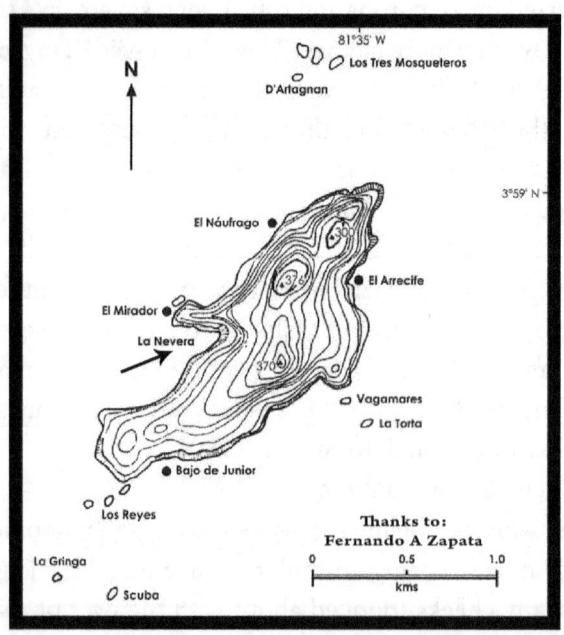

Malpelo Lessons

Malpelo Anchorage

The bay created by the ridge that split into two became little more than a crease in our giant's side. On one side, a vertical wall of dappled grey ran away towards the west. The other side, the arm of the sentinel, fell northwest before crumbling into the sea.

Having furled sails and tidied ropes, when motoring back along the abrupt face Jason shouted, "Look! A cave!"

"And there's another one," I pointed ahead to a vertical split in the rock face with an opening at sea level.

"Over there! Look!" Jude called from the wheel, nodding to the left at another vertical fissure. This much bigger split extended from the sea to the apex of the ridges, towering up as if two phenomenal forces had tried to rip the rock apart.

This gash opened, growing deeper as grey-white walls visually sheared away from the other until what I perceived as the sentinel's arm appeared nearly severed from the central mass.

"Another cave!" cried Judith, getting excited and pointing ahead to the base of this aeons old fissure where another spooky Earth creature's gaping black mouth lay. "Ah, Jack. We've got to stop here," Judith pleaded.

Pointing an extended finger down, Jude knew I wanted to know the depth.

Her head dropped below the dodger's hatch for an instant. When she popped back up, her eyes hardened, her eyebrows furrowed. "Thirty fathoms." She sounded dismayed. "Far too deep to anchor."

"Thirty fathoms, one hundred eighty feet. Damn," I muttered, alarmed, but not giving up. "Let's chug around and sound the bottom. Head over to that flat face near the fissure."

Her eyes shot over to the rock face, and as she watched the swell ride up, her worried face took over. "You want to drive?" She appealed in a way I knew she felt apprehensive. Me too, what a place to screw up.

Though the bay appeared calm, a surge occasionally rounded the corner and drove in with some power. And although protected from the breeze, without warning, sharp gusts blasted down from all directions. This is when adventuring gets serious. We love isolated locations when everything goes well, but one mistake, one failure, then exciting fun can instantly turn into a life-threatening danger.

"Jerome, slacken the anchor and get the gypsy ready to run," I ordered while heading towards the cockpit. "Jason, get the fenders out just in case. Let's be prepared."

Taking the helm, the depth recorder flashed next to the thirty-fathom mark. In no hurry, engaging the gears a few revolutions at a time by applying light pressure on the gear lever, I coaxed our baby closer to the rock. Three boat lengths from its sheer face, the sounder still warned of great depths.

In a hugely enjoyable, tense moment, Malpelo's precipitous slopes formed a remarkable amphitheatre filled with the white tufts of booby birds staring at us. Above and to our left, near the crumbling wrist, a half dozen frigatebirds, black with sinister hooked beaks, peered down watching the show. And right in front of us, an amazing sight. That fissure, cleaved open as if by a mighty sword, ran wide enough for three boats side by side. At its far end, along a tongue of powder blue sea opened a black yawning mouth of another enormous cave. Mystery lay there, perhaps even treasure within its shadows.

Like a lazy water beetle, *Banyandah* drifted atop a transparent sea of great depth judged by the blue darkening ever so slowly as we followed the rock into oblivion. Along the water's edge ran a pink ribbon which on closer inspection became a massive band of limpets. Three fish, each the size of one of my sons, swam between the boat and shore with their gigantic mouths wide open, straining the sea for tiny morsels.

Jude and the boys became enthralled sightseeing shouting from the foredeck whenever they spotted something extra special. Time had little

Malpelo Lessons

meaning while *Banyandah* just drifted with the sounder searching for a pinnacle of bottom, finding none. The bottom dropped away to great depths. Maybe long ago, Malpelo had been a volcano. Millenniums of erosion may have washed the outside away, leaving only this rock, the volcano's plug. The three jagged spires lying offshore could be other vents.

The boys were keen to climb to the peak and I knew Jude particularly enjoys exploring caves, so I needed to find a way to anchor *Banyandah*, if only for the day. A plan came to mind, risky, but worth a go.

"Okay gang, gather round," I said, joining them at the railing. "We're going to drop the anchor then run a stern line ashore."

Jude whipped around. "What! That's crazy. It's much too deep."

"Maybe, but along where that cleft runs into the bay, I got readings of one hundred fifty feet. We anchored deeper than that at Kingman Reef."

Saying that didn't stop Jude. "Yeah and getting our anchor back at Kingman took more than two hours. Or don't you remember?"

My eyebrows shot up remembering that particular morning's anger and frustration. Indeed, Kingman had been tough. Two hundred feet to a sand bottom behind the tiniest, most primitive reef with the nearest help more than a thousand miles away. If we hadn't been on charter, we'd have passed that one by. So I crossed my fingers and hoped this place would be easier.

"Come on, Jude. You want to stop or not? The boys are stronger now, and we'll get our anchor back, I promise."

Jude made no further comment. She wanted to stay but voiced her concern as part of her job keeping me tracking straight.

"Okay, here's the plan. The bottom might be jagged, so we'll buoy the anchor with a stout return line to un-jam it if the anchor gets stuck. You do that, Jude. Tie our mooring lines together until you get a hundred and eighty feet. Jason, Jerome, you launch *Little Scamp* and go scout the shore to the left of that cleft. Search for a hole or lump to tie our stern line onto. Okay? Clear?"

Nods all around.

"Well, let's go."

I moved *Banyandah* out to a safer distance then let her drift while we made preparations. In ten minutes, we were ready. Up and down our foredeck, Jude laid the lines tied together, one end attached to the backside of our anchor, the other to our buoy. *Little Scamp* with the boys rowing two abreast along a mid-ocean shore, searched for a knob that would hold *Banyandah* stern to the rock to prevent her dragging the bow anchor off the undersea cliff face. If that happened, the '*B*' might drift out to sea, or onto other rocks. In either case, we'd lose our baby and be stranded.

With the line ready, I nudged *Banyandah* closer to the boys still searching from about an oar's length of the shore. They looked comical. Side by side, each with a hand on an oar, their other swatting the air around their heads. Malpelo must be plagued with bugs.

After the boys found a stout knob to tie our line onto, I manoeuvred *Banyandah* into position over the undersea slope and backed up towards the face. Judith dropped the bow anchor and paid out chain until the boys could fasten our stern line to the shore. In minutes we were settled, stern to, barely a boat length off the rock face.

Such a beautiful spot, on one side a cave opened while another captured our imagination on the other. As if behind an invisible barrier, wind gusts ceased ruffling the water just in front of us and the swell seemed less as we were tucked nicely into a corner. All well, except for the thousands of bugs. Small midges with transparent wings and slender bodies, taking great pleasure in crawling over our arms and legs, getting caught in our hair. Strange, they didn't bite, just a darn nuisance.

"Shall we eat lunch early?" Jude asked, "It's ready."

"Sure, I'm starved." Cupping hands towards the mountain, I sang out "Jason! Jerome! Lunch!" Hearing the echo, I thought what a strange call to bounce off these walls.

With Malpelo towering straight up, we gathered around the cockpit table now spread with freshly baked bread and the crispy fried Rainbow Runner we'd caught earlier, along with other delights to celebrate a first meal at anchor. When the initial chomping and hunger eased Jason commented that he'd seen the strangest lizard. That reminded me of seeing him, after he'd tied our rope to shore, sitting quietly on a rock platform overlooking the bay. He'd been so still, I'd thought him lost in thought or entranced by a school of fish feeding along the shore. Malpelo possessed that unique quality of something special always in sight.

Jason described the reptile using his finger to outline its shape. "He was all black with a wavy frill, like a rooster's comb sprouting from his head." Then he grinned, shaking his head in wonder. "There are lots of them. And boy, are they curious. I sat very still, and several walked right up to me. One even licked my foot. And guess what? He had the brightest red tongue!" Eyes wide, excitement racing through his voice.

"A bright red tongue?" Jude repeated as she forked another mouthful of the juicy white fish.

"Yeah, and another one, sort of greenish-grey had lots of little yellow spots all over its body. Gosh! And really active, jumping rock to rock."

After lunch, the boys took Judith off to explore the caves while I cleared up the dishes. One of us needed to stay on the boat. We wouldn't feel comfortable leaving our baby unattended. A broken line, a dragged anchor, we didn't want to spend the rest of what would be a rather short life sleeping with the birds and crabs on this rock.

I kept them in sight most of the hour away, except when they stole around a corner to enter one of the sea level caves. When they returned, they climbed on board soaking wet.

First over the railing came Jason, shaking his head and gibbering, "Jeepers, that was creepy."

"Oh, it was not," Judith retorted. "A few small birds darted in and out the cave, some big swell and lots of noise, but not much else."

Jerome, who had been securing *Little Scamp* to the stern, climbed on board. "Tell Dad about the fresh water."

"Fresh water?" I asked, "What fresh water?"

"That cave over there," she said, pointing towards the hidden one, "has water dripping across its entrance. Maybe rainwater percolating down."

I looked at the grey rock that separated the hole from us, "Fresh? You're sure?"

"Sure, I'm sure. I tasted it. That's why we're wet."

"Perhaps an artesian spring from deep in the Earth. From how high did it drip?"

"What do you think Jerome, ten metres?" she asked, pointing to a spot on the mast approximating that height.

An expert opinion requested, Jerome put on his pensive demeanour, and somewhere in his grey matter, an exact measurement was being calculated. No one rushed him. More enjoyable watching the mind of this young adventurer tumble than needing the answer.

"Ah..." he uttered, thought lines straightening out, "About ten metres, maybe a bit more." Then he gave a final authoritative nod.

A chuckle escaped me before I could stop it.

"What?" my growing space engineer asked. "What's wrong?"

I smiled again and gave his arm a playful squeeze.

"Oh, nothing. You're just cute, that's all."

With no explanation for the curtain of fresh water, we set in motion our next event; an assault of the summit. Canvas walking shoes got dug out of storage, a container filled with fruit drink, the camera checked for film, and last, I wrote our names and address plus a few details about our visit on a piece of paper and sealed the message in a bottle for placing at the tippy-top. One last necessary measure, coating ourselves with bug repellent.

In a critical manoeuvre, timed to the swell fluctuating half a man's height, Judith rode the swell in, back rowing till *Little Scamp* crunched the wall where for a moment it hovered at the top. In a wink, whoever's turn sprang across onto jagged spikes and sharp limpets. One slip and those crustaceans would slice open flesh. The next instant, the yellow dinghy dropped while Jude pulled a few deft strokes to get away with the run of swell. Not an exercise for beginners.

Once assembled on the rock with shoes and daypacks in place, we took off—straight up! On toes, and using hands, we inched up, climbing the rock face until reaching the first plateau. *Banyandah's* masthead now lay far below. Down even further, a miniature Judith, a hand shading her face, gave a wave sending us on our way.

We climbed to the extreme end of that plateau where, feeling puffed, I stopped to enjoy the lovely sight of a blue upon blue world in every direction. Radiating towards us marched an army of sparkling silver wind ripples created by the afternoon sun reflecting off their crests. Above them, white fluffy clouds hung motionless as if dabbled on a canvas of cornflower blue.

Looking closer, boobies nested everywhere on the pebble-strewn ground. Some guarded a single white egg with brownish-purple speckles. Others, frail featherless chicks under them. None seemed frightened by us. In fact, when approached slowly, those without eggs or chicks would allow us within an arm's reach. But we didn't touch them. Some wild animals might allow humans close, but they don't like to be touched.

The boobies squatting upon an egg or chicks didn't react so placidly. Instead, they grew visibly nervous upon our approach. When still several metres away they would turn their heads to one side and dip their beak as if pecking the ground. Then they'd quarter turn the other way and dip it again. If we moved closer, they rummaged through the few twigs in their nest. Grasping one crosswise in their bill they'd repeat their warning, striking the ground with the end of the twig as if marking their territory. I can't explain why, but boobies have the most expressive eyes. They don't change shape, and nearly impossible to see them blink, but somehow those perfectly round discs transmitted their pleas, and we always left them unmolested.

Those black lizards with a top frill that Jason described were about. So too the greenish-grey ones with yellow spots. While the frilly lizards looked something out a Japanese sci-fi film, some skinny grey ones jumped rock to rock and pitched up at our feet where they'd freeze. Then zap! They'd snap their head up like a spring-loaded pop-up to look us straight in the eye. Again all movement would cease like a statue except for a pulsating beat in their necks. Next instant, they'd bob their head up and down twice or thrice before a pink tongue came out to lick our skin before rock hopping at breakneck speed, leaving us wondering what the heck?

The dry grainy rocks also housed big slow-moving scaly lizards that in my youth we called Gila monsters. Probably not a very accurate name for these creatures as I don't think they're the same venomous ones of America. Their blunt heads, rounded bodies to stumpy tails were covered with dark scales large enough to identify as individual hard pads stuck onto leathery skin, and fat like the Gila monsters I'd known years ago. Unlike their skinny cousins, these lethargic fatsoes weren't curious. They preferred to remain inert in the shade under the larger boulders. But as Jason found, their bloated shape is deceiving for they can move with surprising speed if approached.

We slogged higher and higher under a warm, lowering sun, tripping over sharp stones sometimes losing foothold on crumbling boulders. When halfway up, Malpelo looked one chunk of rock with bits and pieces broken free. Perhaps breccia or a loose conglomerate with a pattern. I'm far from an expert. All I know is that Malpelo's external appearance morphed through several changes during our two-hour ascent. From a solid homogeneous mass near the water's edge to a plateau of crumbly stuff a third of the way up. Next, we came to the ridge forming the sentinel's arm, which ran up to a saddle linked to Malpelo's dome-shaped top. That formation appeared composed of basalt as if this bit of the mountain had been forged crystal by crystal.

One side of the ridge dropped to rocks awash hundreds of feet below. On the other, on *Banyandah's* side, a slide of small stones seemed ready to tumble ended in a drop right above the mouth of the big cave. Lose our footing one way, we'd fall to the sea. Slip the other, we'd tumble in an avalanche and fall smack onto the tongue of the cave. Either way would be deadly. Cautioning the boys, we continued climbing the ridge till we came to the fissure that nearly split the ridge from the main body. There, a dubious rock bridge spanned the crack full of jagged spikes. Having gotten that far, the route ahead looked clear to the shoulder. So, Jerome being the lgihtest, I held onto his hand in an acrobatic lock grip then sent him to test the strength of the bridge.

Loose stones crumbled off and cascaded down in puffs of dust that flew away on the breeze. But the stone bridge held. Unlocking our grip, in two steps Jerome went over. Mincing my actions as if a danseur noble barely touching the stage, I started fine, but wind buffeted me midway. Stopping to regain balance, looking down, I can confirm that the fault all but split the ridge with nasty spears directly below.

Once on the other side, we arrived at the base of the crown, feeling pretty chuffed. Looking up, the top appeared as if an upturned saucepan of solid rock that rose vertically out of loose stones on all but one side. That side rose straight out the ocean like sliced cheese.

From this height, cloud shadows drifted over a vast expanse of steel-grey sea still dappled with shimmering silver brushed by the artist. At the base of the saucepan lay a loose rock incline and our high spirits feeling mischievous, a young man's challenge didn't wait for a reply. Sweating freely, we scrambled, racing each other up that slope, creating an avalanche of sliding stone as we struggled. Through ragged breath we taunted one another, and for a while, it looked bitter defeat for me. But the vitality of youth still lacked the older man's cunning and laughing, and still jeering we breasted the saddle, almost, but not quite in line.

Jason and I were bent over, when Jerome gasped, "What a good race."

A few further words of banter passed between us until we felt the cooling breeze and noticed the abrupt new vista of open sea. The bold weather side of Malpelo now before us, we faced the south wind and straw-coloured cliffs dulled by soft shadows meeting crashing white breakers from faraway. Leaning back trying to slow my breath, sweeping an eye up this sheer face I discovered brown boobies made this rugged weather side their home. Their larger size requires a cliff face or flow of wind to get airborne. Many of these larger birds roosted precariously on narrow ledges, their nesting sites not as secure as the white boobies on the rubble-strewn slopes just passed. How they minded their egg or coped with their young started our heads shaking in wonder. As compensation for their awkward nesting sites, they need only to spread their two-metre wings to gain flight even in this gentle wind.

After a rest, one false start trying to scale the summit's vertical wall using pockmarks for handholds soon became so precarious we gave it away. Luckily, we found a more accessible route up a boulder-strewn fault line wide enough for us to scramble. Up this pathway, we scampered over small rocks right to the tippy top to find Malpelo's bald head almost flat. Walking to the edge of the drop-off, my toes began tingling as if atop the Eiffel Tower just as a sudden wind blast tested my balance.

Malpelo Landing

Daredevil Ridge

Malpelo Lessons

Malpelo Summit Cerro de la Mona

If one day you find yourself on top of *Cerro de la Mona* at a height of 980 feet, you will notice that the horizon bends, not just ahead as seen off any coast, but everywhere around, encircling you. The clouds arch forward from the other side of the planet, and the ocean is almost pregnant in its curvature. Then you'll get a sense of just where you are; atop a rock in the centre of a vast ocean.

Jason went off exploring and found the remnants of a flag on the highest point. Just tatters of faded cloth, yellow, blue, and red, the colours of Colombia hanging off a pole bent over by a past windstorm. Nothing else marked Malpelo's top.

Ceremoniously we placed the bottle containing our note at the flag's base, each of us speculating on how long before another human would stand upon this isolated spot. While doing this, my gaze drifted to the far horizon and with heartfelt gratitude for the love of life coursing through me, chanted my thanks to the creator.

Snug in a spot on Malpelo's quiet northern edge, the three of us snuggled close while our muscles recovered. Looking down upon the expanse of sea just sailed upon, our egos soared, revelling in achieving our goal. Significantly impacted by having pure Nature surrounding us catapulted my mind through events witnessed in my short life.

Our day filled with Nature not tarnished by humankind sent my mind into chaos thinking over the extreme events coming to Earth. A false world is emerging and coming fast. Only in isolated locations like Malpelo do wild creatures live unrestricted and free. Humans are spreading as if a cancer across the planet, bringing an increasing need for housing and employment that requires land-clearing and building.

As these thoughts boiled up within me, I gave Jerome and Jason's arms a gentle squeeze.

"Remember last summer when we toured Europe, the incident on the Eiffel Tower waiting in the long queue, and again at the Vatican? The big crowds, the pushing, how it got out of control?"

"Hmm." Jerome snuggled closer, his chuckle coming through in his voice. "I remember you standing on the railing, telling that stampede to play fair and remain human."

Visions of those crowds switched to images of cities we'd recently visited. Mauritius appeared a patchwork of neatly divided allotments jammed with humanity struggling to survive. Africa, with little forest remaining, very different from our honeymoon in the sixties. Europe already carpeted with human life, only China limiting births, but far too late. Everywhere else, we create babies at an increasing rate. In many places, religious groups race one another to maintain their power base. Cultural groups do the same. More produces more.

My head, by its own volition, began to wag side to side. Who to blame? Old people wanted to live to the fullest last instant. Young people had a right to experience the love of their own children. And humanity is supremely concerned with human life.

Developed economies require growth even though we live in a finite world. Constant growth requires more and more babies, and that coupled with the religious zealots means today's society is having problems even talking about reining in the runaway explosion of people needing resources. We never hear 'reduce world population.' Any politician suggesting that would be out of a job.

How odd for these thoughts in a location where I could scream my voice hoarse, and no one would hear.

"Boys, you've heard this from me before, my speaking about fossil fuel emissions, nuclear waste, and the million pollutants created by too many people. Globally we're gobbling up great tracts of land, altering the Earth to the detriment of the wild kingdom. As a result, we're creating a new form of human life; a breed isolated from Nature, a population that only knows things created by man, where the rest of Earth is secondary knowledge from visions on a screen or in a zoo or museum.

"The one truth is the wonder, majesty, and power of Earth and creation of life. Humans are unique for a reason, and it's not to dominate, but to find harmony and balance within the creation so we can become one with its secrets. Perhaps then we'll attain the higher knowledge needed to understand the why? To reach universal nirvana, we need to tolerate each individual's religious explanations and together worship Earth as tangible evidence of a force far more significant than our mortal souls. When we do that, we'll understand the how and why."

We'd been sitting on a natural rock shelf near the tattered flag, overlooking a sea marked in parallel arcs that sparkled in the lowering sun. Intertwined in pure peace, in an instant our mood was shattered by a new sound. Encroaching into our world came a hum, an unchanging dull sound that took a few moments to place.

I cocked my head to the wind. "Listen, do you hear what I hear?"

Jerome jumped to his feet. "A ship!" he exclaimed.

Jason jumped up too. "Yeah, I hear it too."

Getting up, my legs stiff. "Where? Do you see it?"

With a three hundred sixty degree view of an empty blue world, locating the new arrival took no more than a few seconds.

"There!" Jason shouted. "Past that point, about a mile out." And he stretched his arm towards the far end of the sentinel's back.

Sure enough, a tuna-fishing boat, easily identified by its peculiar fishing rig and huge power block that hauls in the big net.

"I'll be damned!" I began. "A whole bloody ocean and we still can't be alone."

I wasn't actually disappointed. In fact, I felt excited and curious as the fishing boat rounded the ridge to pass the indentation where *Banyandah* lay. But there its low hum slowed, which got me wondering whether they wanted to anchor in the same bay. Realising there'd not be sufficient room created a natural concern for the safety of my ship.

"We'd better get back," I said softly, not to alarm the boys. "I don't know what that fellow's up to, but I'd rather be back on board."

"Think they're pirates?" Jason joked.

"Nah. But better to be on board if he tries to squeeze into our nook."

Although I'd replied casually, Jason's remark struck home. Jude was alone far below.

"Let's go," I ordered.

Finding the trail down looked quite different from coming up. The rocks didn't seem quite in the same place, and we missed the fissure we'd used. Unknowingly, we claimed a new route. One that became steeper and less sure as we groped our way down the same windward edge. And while we tumbled and slid, the *Banyandah* and her mysterious visitor remained blocked from sight. That made us hurry even more until we stumbled into a blind end. Having to go back up set worrisome thoughts creeping round my head, adding more tension, so every time I lost grip, I had to caution myself, Don't rush.

The second route we chose wasn't the right one either. It tumbled down another split that ended in a challenging toe and finger traverse across a sheer face. Taking that, forced us to use cracks and tiny handholds above a house high drop onto a jumble of rocks.

The boys sized it up in a flash and sped across in one fluid motion. They were already on their way across the rubble slope when I arrived, out of breath and sweating freely.

To be an explorer, skills are continually challenged. Not accepting those challenges is to not experience places like Malpelo. Sure, there are dangers. But they can be judged and prepared for. Not the blind danger of a B-double coming across a double-white line.

Alone, I looked down, and my fingertips tingled. A flash of heat brought sweat. I thought of a more comfortable life—a house, car. I thought about turning back to try another route. Then, I blasted myself. "Get on with it. Where's that courage you hold so high?"

I tested one foot then started stepping out, handhold, toehold, dry rock against my face. Suddenly across and racing like a gazelle fleeing a lion.

Catching up with the boys at the base of the saucepan, we saw the tuna boat now adrift off our bay. On its aft deck, half a dozen men in action, slid a large tender into the sea.

My stomach flipped thinking of Judith, alone and unprotected hundreds of feet below, Jason's remark haunting me in a series of bad thoughts: Colombia; rumours of pirates; a lone yacht; an unprotected woman.

"Let's move, guys," I urged. "But be careful. An accident up here and we're in trouble."

Sliding down the loose slope, stones cascaded before us. Reaching the ridgeline boulder hopping like I used to do in dry riverbeds, without hesitation scurrying across the rock bridge that we'd first thought so dangerous, then along the knife-edge with white surf far below.

The large tender began moving with a band of five onboard towards the calmer water of our cove. We went faster. Down the spine, boobies flopped out our way. As we ran, the tender approached *Banyandah* until both vessels disappeared behind a lump yet to get around.

Play it cool Jack. Everything will be okay, my mind kept saying as five minutes passed, then ten, and thankfully no screams or shots rang out. In fact, no sounds except the distant hum of machinery and the intake of my breath. Already wet from hard work, I became even more so remembering the rape and murder stories spread on the yachting grapevine.

At last, we dropped onto the plateau and scurried to its edge, my heart pounding as much from exertion as concern. *Banyandah's* masthead came into view, followed by her decks. Beside her lay the tender. Not right alongside, but drifting a few feet away with the five dark-haired men still on board. They were engrossed in conversation with Judith, who sat on *Banyandah's* foredeck with her legs dangling over the side.

"You-hoo! Mum! We're back." Jason's call echoed around the hills, causing boobies and frigates to turn their heads. So did the men. Judith waved.

Fifteen minutes later, we were home. A few scratches, one cut, and two dozen photos; the sum total of our ascent. When Judith came to ferry us back, the tender moved toward one of the caves. So while the boys babbled on about their mountaintop adventures, Jude commented on her visitors. We all seemed to be talking at once.

"They're Ecuadorians. From the port of Manta." She informed me after the hubbub died. "One of them speaks English. Says he lived in California for a short time."

What good luck. Here's a chance to get some local knowledge on the ports and coastline of Ecuador. So, while I cleaned up, I kept a lookout for the tender, ready to call them alongside. In minutes my chance came, and moments later, I'm shaking hands with Ramando, the skipper of the *Intrepid*. Pleasant-looking, his nut-brown face and deep crows feet marked him a man of the sea. When I shook his hand, I found his palm and fingers rough with calluses. Eagerly I invited him aboard. It took a bit of coaxing, but he came, first wiping his bare feet with a rag found tucked in the corner of his tender.

He wouldn't take any drink, not even a glass of water. Only the boy, his son aged about nine accepted a juice. His crew also declined. Gentle people these, more afraid of offending than ever causing harm, like most of the world's people.

In a flash, I dug out the charts of Ecuador and explained that we were heading to Guayaquil to collect mail, but that afterwards, we needed a secure place to leave our vessel while we travelled inland.

He and his crew talked this over in Spanish, and although I knew a few words of their language, most everything escaped me. Speaking in broken English, Ramando described Guayaquil as a large commercial port. He recommended Manta as the best place.

"Manta has a *yate club*," he said beaming a proud smile, "*es tranquilo*."

Pointing to the enlargement of Manta on our chart, I asked should we go inside what looked like a circular breakwater which itself lay within a sea wall. By his confused face, I guessed he'd never seen a chart of Manta before.

More chatter between him and his crew followed my query then he said "*Si*, that's the place."

Well, that looked fine to me, in fact just what we wanted. Wondering about the depth as the chart didn't detail that enclosed area, even though Ramando said we could go there, sometimes boatmen don't know of a yacht's deep keel and our need for a tall man's depth of water. Standing up straight, I asked about the depth while pointing from my feet to well above my head.

Again a buzz of Spanish, followed by, "*Si*, four or five metres at least."

"Okay, that's great!" and I grinned just like a kid given a lolly, and extended my hand, "*Gracias*."

I asked if he'd like to look below. So many others around the world have been curious about our floating home. But, he declined, indicating with his large hands that he wasn't cleanly dressed.

"Nonsense," I said, motioning him to follow and stepped through the forward companionway.

He held back with an appealing shy look, so odd on such a weather-beaten face, only leaping forward like a cat after his crew chided him. Once below, his face softened, immediately struck by the homey compactness of *Banyandah*. I left him gawking at the fixtures and bric-à-brac collected around the world to invite his son to join us too. After that, one by one, the entire crew came below. Four rough fishermen and a boy, looking, pointing, jabbering in Spanish. I really enjoy moments like those, taking delight in sharing some of the uniqueness of our sailing life.

Malpelo Lessons

That just about sums up our adventure at Malpelo. Ramando and his 'motley' crew, for they were several races, left straight after their tour. Directly after that, we set to work reclaiming our anchor from Malpelo's great depths. I'm not tooting my horn, but the gear came up with hardly a fuss.

Ramando and his *Intrepid* came to see us on our way, and as we motored out the bay, both crews lined the railings, shouting bon voyage.

Then as the sun touched the curved horizon seen so clearly from *Cerro de la Mona*, we hoisted sails. And in the light puffs from Malpelo's lofty peak, *Banyandah* silently drifted towards the sentinel's far point where a fair breeze caught her sails giving our lady life.

Like the ending of many a good story, we set off toward the distant horizon in search of new adventures, a blazing fire-red tropical sunset behind us. In its centre, framed by those magnificent colours of Nature, the soaring dome of that mid-ocean rock stood black and proud, challenging all with its might. Goodbye Malpelo, none of us will ever forget your magnificence.

Footnote: The Turning Point

To bring you up to date on our rocky friend Malpelo, this happened after arriving back in Australia.

Remember our last sighting Malpelo tall and proud against a blaze of tropical wonder. After leaving her, we sailed another ten thousand miles. In fact, over the next nine months, we crossed the entire Pacific Ocean before seeing the name Malpelo again. That happened in Coffs Harbour, just a few days after completing our world circumnavigation, Christmas 1986.

The *Four J's,* are in a tight knot inside *Banyandah's* saloon, excitedly sorting through the first mail received in many months, containing letters from family and friends with stamps from around the world. From out the stack dropped a buff packet about the size of a photo envelope, its outside chopped by a half dozen rubber-stamps.

Express - Entrada Inmediata, one noted in red ink.

Another, declared in blue, *Presidencia de la Republica*

"Wow! A letter from the President," Jason reached to read the ink chops more easily.

Jerome grabbed the other corner saying, "Can I have the stamps?"

Reflections in a Sailor's Eyes

Pulling the envelope free, turning it over, I read the return address: Colonel Jaime Alberto Escoba Garzon, Casa Militar Presidencia, Bogota, Colombia.

Giving that little thought, I was still trying to work out the *Presidencia* stamp, wondering how it pertained to us.

Standing in the saloon, a boy hanging onto each arm and Judith looking over my shoulder, I slit open the envelope and extracted a crisp white letter decorated across the top with "Presidencia de la Republica." Also enclosed, wrapped within the folds of the message, a short stack of photos and a postcard. The card showed a naval ship with a helicopter hovering over it.

Handing the card to Jason, we saw that the top photo showed mostly the sky. At its bottom, a few crumbly, shat upon rocks with some part of an orange-painted structure half cut off on the picture's right. Mid-photo, five dark-skinned men in shorts and light shirts stood at ease under a flapping yellow, blue, and red Colombian flag.

The next photo showed the entire structure from a different angle. A simple light structure, fabricated from steel angles with a large glass dome on its top and a solar cell to power the light attached to its side.

These photos were sending our curiosity spinning, and with more in hand, I flicked to the next shot.

Straightaway we saw a military scene with a helicopter in flight dangling some kind of load in a cargo net. Hovering over rocky ground above a circle with an 'H' at its centre, all in white. The sea behind the helipad appeared smooth, its surface darker stretching to a misted horizon, where upon the sea sat naval ships, one clearly loading another helicopter with gear.

"Malpelo!" yelled Jerome.

Could it be, I thought, quickly flipping to the next photo.

Yes, Malpelo, because once again we saw the tumbled grey rocks cascading down centuries-old slopes. But the central theme of this photo showed some sort of formal ceremony going on. Two military men dressed smartly in khaki uniforms stood at attention alongside a single civilian dressed in tropical white. More military sporting green and brown fatigues formed ranks behind those three. Even more people filled the background; some wore white uniforms, others carried camera gear and still others in ordinary dress.

Malpelo Lessons

But the real show stopper wasn't the thirty or forty humans on the island. No, what made our eyes pop wide was the sight of a medium-sized building erected next to the helipad.

Astonishing! On what had been unaltered slopes since creation, and now, since our visit a few months ago, stood a pointy-roofed building looking complete and ready for action.

OH, NO! exploded in my mind while the Jude muttered expletives.

With more than a tad bit of disbelief, turning to the next shot, we saw what must have been early days in the construction. Only one ship on the sea, the rocks of the island littered with piles of lumber, cast pieces of concrete, drums and other fitments and a few men standing about the building site. In the corner of the photo a solitary booby bird, and the only one in any of the pictures. He seemed to be watching the activities with a curious look as if wondering what it meant.

The last of the photos must have been taken from one of the ships and showed Malpelo's brooding dark shape standing clear against pale light dominated by one massive cloud. In every direction the sea calm and grey-blue, sparkling like the day of our visit.

That one image brought back a flood of warm memories, and for a few moments, we remained silent. Until broken from behind by Judith's earnest voice, "Read the letter, Jack. Let's hear what they've done."

>Bogata, May 30th
>Dear Friends,
>I was very pleased to find the message that you left at the Malpelo Island on April 8, on your way from Panama to Ecuador.
>From April 14, many changes have taken place on the island. In fact, under the instructions of President Betancur, this point of Colombian territory has become a useful and practical place. We have built, among other installations, a guiding light, a house, a meteorological station, a heliport and so on. From that date, we have settled a naval base for the Colombian Navy. In order to give you a better idea about the present condition of the Malpelo Island, I enclose herewith some late pictures of the Island, some of which were taken during an official trip several weeks ago...
>Colonel Escobar
>Presidency of the Republic

"Gosh, only six days after we left," Jason exclaimed.

The shortage of time between the two visits didn't strike me as strongly as the very deed—'among other installations...' and 'a naval base for...' stuck in my craw.

Passing the letter to Jude, I thumbed back through the photos, thinking, Why the heck does man have to invade every place? What about the thousands of birds that have made Malpelo their breeding spot since the beginning of time? Now we've made a toe hold on their mid-ocean rock!

"This point of Colombian territory... has become a useful and practical place."

A thousand foot high mid-ocean rock just a mile in length, Nature's needs are far more useful and practical than man's. Yes, I know, such a tiny step; only one small house. But it's the FIRST step. Like Neil Armstrong said, "One small step for man - One giant leap for mankind." Well, what about Nature? To blazes with man thinking only about mankind.

Twenty years after our visit to Isla Malpelo, on 12 July 2006, UNESCO declared Malpelo a World Heritage fauna and flora sanctuary and a Colombian foundation is trying to preserve the biodiversity of the site. But by 2010, Malpelo had become a critically acclaimed dive site and also counted as a separate entity for amateur radio contact. This prompted an urgent request that same year to establish an adequate waste treatment system in the Malpelo fauna and flora sanctuary. And to provide coast guard training in the prevention of invasive species arriving at the island. Sound familiar?

As the world's population doubles, then triples, what do you think will happen to the thousands of seabirds that have raised their chicks on this isolated mid-ocean rock? And what will happen to their food source?

HENRY'S BOO-BOO

Here's a bit of gossip that I know to be true and a perfect example of what I mean when I say cruising yachtsmen have to be clever with their hands as well as their minds. It's an example of what can happen if you hang on to your city thinking out in Nature's world.

Enter one gentleman named Henry, not his real name, but it'll do to save the poor fellow any further embarrassment, and his dear wife, Sweetie Pie, plus one kitty-cat named, for want of another, Sassy. Keen sailors, one and all, having sailed around their hometown waters on weekend jaunts, and loving it. The sailor's life is really living both think. So they toss normal life, sell the house and board an aircraft that takes them halfway around the world to France where they purchase their dream-come-true sailing machine, taking delivery of it just like Mr. Smith down the street would slip into a factory fresh cherry red Mustang.

After that, for Henry and wife, kitty-cat too, it's what comes naturally. They put to sea. And soon letters back home begin to smack of little adventures, like an encounter with the blunt end of a wharf, a misplaced buoy that ran them aground, and a sky filled with nasty black clouds that wouldn't go away when rocks lay hidden in their murk. But through it all, their letters always closed with the same happy line: "Life's great. Love to all."

Quite soon for Captain Henry and Sweetie Pie crew, the Mediterranean came to an end and their first big water stretched before them. With a gulp and all fingers crossed, they pointed their new sailing craft towards the bleak unknown. And with a zoom, swish, and splash and a few *yippees* thrown in they arrived at the other end of the Atlantic in about a month's time. Naturally with a long list of do's and don'ts ready for the next time.

Then for this happy crew, it was a hippety-hop through one chain of islands after another. Until, sooner than that they thought, along comes the next ocean.

Now here's where the *Four J's* first met these newly initiated cruising folk. You see, somewhere in their travels, someone had told them that amateur radio was the way to stay in touch with a world left behind. So just before setting off across the world's largest ocean, they bought one. And in a rush, it got screwed down in an unused corner of their yacht, and then away they went. Next stop, the South Pacific Ocean.

Our first meeting with Henry and crew came via the airways. They were three days out from the Galapagos bound for the Marquises, while we were halfway down the same ocean, heading for Easter Island, the island of statues. During our first brief QSO (that's ham talk for a conversation), we basically just introduced ourselves, described our boats and shared a bit of chatter on where we were bound and what we were up to. Two other yachts, both with amateur radio on board, were 'on air' at the same time and as one happened to be an old friend of ours, a daily chat session was suggested. These 'at sea' radio chats are something like the olden day gathering of washer women over the back fence, a good place to idle away some of the tedious hours of crossing oceans, swap fish stories or share the latest horror story.

On that passage, we had two days of: "Oh, isn't the weather super." And: "We landed another fish this morning." Until, on day three, Henry's titbit floored us all. His extraordinary news, relayed through the ether in a subdued hesitating voice, was that they'd run out of cooking gas that morning. No, not just run out of one tank, but run out completely. With something like three weeks of empty ocean before their next bit of land, they had no fuel to cook with. Nothing to boil water for that mandatory cuppa before taking the early morning watch. What a disaster! Call out search and rescue! Better still, start praying for a passing ship.

Now, it's pretty hard to ask over a radio the kind of questions you'd like to when it comes to something as stupid as that. Hard, unless you don't mind your words sounding like finger pointing. I mean, someone on board must have slipped up. But, I had to do it. My curiosity just wouldn't be contained, so I blurted out, "Didn't you check your gas bottles before leaving port?" To wit the collected group of listening yachtsmen, and possibly hundreds of shore stations as well, heard a rather long-winded account detailing their every movement prior to

Henry's Boo-Boo

setting sail. All interspersed by a whole bunch of 'ums' and 'aahs' that painted a pretty good picture of Captain Henry's embarrassment.

Basically it all boiled down to: Yes, their gas cylinders had been checked. One had been half full, and the other had been empty. So that one had been passed onto the Panama Yacht Club for refilling. As per usual, everything had been hurry, hurry, "we're just about to leave." So somehow, another soul from the club had delivered the gas cylinder back on board Henry's ship. And Henry, finding it there upon his return from the club bar where he'd had a few last minute drinks, put it below just before casting off.

Like Henry said, "I assumed it had been filled."

Three weeks later, after a short passage and some days in the Galapagos Islands, they were three days into a very long voyage when the original half tank of gas ran out.

"The old tank went out this morning," we heard Henry say. "I flicked over to the other. But there was nothing."

Gulp! All of us around our radios swallowed hard with the thought of no cooked food for several weeks.

Hearing Henry's explanation, my reaction was what a foolhardy mistake. But then Jude reminded me of a similar experience we'd had several years earlier. So when it came again my turn to speak, I tried to make Henry feel less foolish by relating how we'd once done the very same thing.

"Once I filled my second gas bottle using a friend's car." I started out, speaking across the ocean via the amateur radio in *Banyandah's* aft cabin. "Filled it in Perth, Western Australia, where they do that sort of thing at petrol stations. My mistake was that I went to the hardware store next door while the attendant filled the cylinder. And, as we later discovered, he'd only half filled it. Normally I'd have known by the tank's light weight. But not that time. It was loaded into the car for me, then at the other end, my kids hefted it out and put it in place on the deck. Two weeks later, in the middle of a wet stormy winter crossing of the Australian Bight, we ran out of gas."

In our case, we were more fortunate than Henry. Our cold diet was forced upon us for only two days. The first port we passed, we pulled in. But poor Henry and Sweetie-Pie wife were faced with weeks of it. After my monologue, the collected group of yachtsmen at the ends of their microphones began pouring forth sympathy and good ideas: "Oh you poor dears, soak your rice for a few hours then put it in the sun." Click. "No, put it on top of your engine when it's running." Click. "Grow your beans into sprouts." Click. "Get to like raw fish." Click. "Better still soak the fish in lemon juice." And I suggested they use their kerosene lantern to heat a tin of water for that morning cup of coffee just as I had years earlier. Morning coffee is pretty important to me.

Well, day after day, their ordeal went on and on and on, just like some ocean passages tend to do. And as it did, their initial courage and brash front slipped little by little. I guess the cheese and biscuit and cold canned pea diet wore a bit thin. As a result, their radio contacts became fewer. No, not from weakness, though heavens above they must have lost weight. But probably it just got a bit monotonous our parading their hunger right out in front of them with our kind enquires. Besides, when floating about in the middle of an ocean, what else can you talk about except freshly baked bread, banana cakes, and pancakes for breakfast.

What compounded their plight was that they were catching a lot of fish - big ones -juicy, fine tasting Tuna and Dorado. Lovely food, except they said they couldn't get over the fact that it was uncooked. Lucky Sassy, she got the lot and must have gotten fat.

Days passed, slowly, so too the miles. We arrived at Easter Island. Henry and crew arrived at French Polynesia, and so I'm told, tucked into a mammoth feast moments after landing. Imagine them rowing ashore at top speed then a quick look one-way then the other for the nearest restaurant. Then a burst of speed down the beach to the nearest hotel. Zoom! Straight into the dining room shouting, "No menu - Just bring us food - HOT food!"

The very next day, Henry bought the biggest tank of cooking gas on the island. End of story. Or so I thought. But yesterday, many weeks after the event, while I was communicating via my little cube of electronic wonder, I heard the closing sequel. And it's a beauty. I was on air with one of the other boats who had shared in their misadventure and I brought up Henry's name.

"Where's Henry? What's he up to?" I asked. "I haven't heard a thing since the cooking gas fiasco."

Moments later, my friend's reply knocked me off my radio chair and sent *Banyandah* rocking with laughter. It seems Henry's new Zip-a-Dee-

Henry's Boo-Boo

Doo-Dah sailing machine had one of those new-beaut electric safety valves on the gas line. The ones that are closed when de-activated. In other words: Flick the switch, power on, the valve opens and you can cook. Flick again, power off, and the gas flow shuts off. A great safety device because we all know how explosive cooking gas can be on a yacht. But here's the punch line which I'll bet you've already guessed. Henry's electrical goody had burnt out! Flick the switch, nothing happened, except maybe, "Dear, we're out of gas."

And when he switched over to the other cylinder.... Flick, still not a thing.

But, yep. Henry had gas all those long miles across the Pacific, a full cylinder of the stuff. Enough to cook hundreds of cakes and all those fish. Oodles of it to heat their rice and create all sorts of culinary delights to while away the long hours of blue ocean.

Poor Henry! If he'd been clever in mind as well as clever with his hands, he could have had it all. Which proves you can't take city thinking out to sea because there just aren't any servicemen out there.

I would have loved being a bug on the bulkhead when he gave that news to Sweetie Pie wife.

Jerome navigating Banyandah around the world

Reflections in a Sailor's Eyes

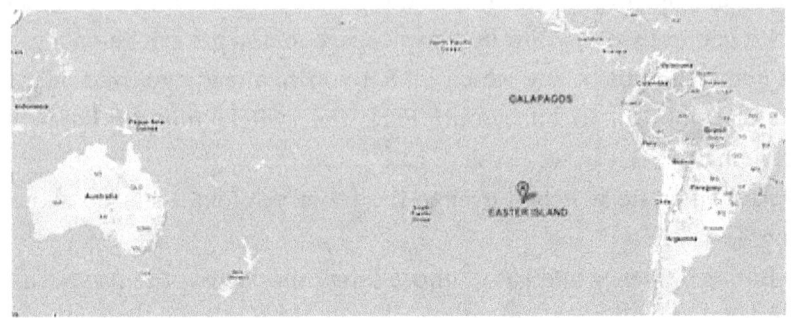

Voyage Panama, Ecuador, Galapagos, Easter Island

Rapa Nui, Easter Island the land of statues
Ahu Ature Huki - Anakena and the original statue raised by the Heyerdahl expedition

TO THE NAVEL OF THE WORLD

"You're on your way where? To Easter Island! Wow, that'll be great!" Harry Mead's voice, sounding awed and impressed, came loud and clear over the Ham radio in *Banyandah's* aft cabin. "But isn't this the wrong time of year?" Scepticism had crept into his voice. "You know it is winter down there."

Of course, I knew. When planning this voyage, I'd sat for hours with our dog-eared weather charts, tracking over and again July's wind patterns for the South Pacific. Harry voiced his worry over storms, but storms weren't shown in the ocean north of Easter Island. Frustrating calms and wind from around the clock would challenge us.

The crash and bang of drooping sails now confirmed what those charts showed. Again we were becalmed—the sails on a starvation ration. Our fourth straight night without wind and we're bobbing about like a toy boat in a bathtub with storms from the deep Southern Ocean sending us a fury of swell. In the last twenty-four days, *Banyandah* has managed a mere eighteen hundred miles—a jellyfish could go faster! A measly one hundred miles separates us from the island of statues—perhaps we should motor.

> Jerome's Journal: 24 June 1986
> Anchors up and we're off to visit the statues of Easter Island. That is if we can make it. Dad says it is a nineteen hundred mile voyage to the island, and some of this voyage will be through variable winds.

> Jerome's Journal: 3 July 1986
> For the first eight days, we did well, averaging about one hundred twenty miles a day on a 215° course. During that time, we caught four dorado fish and one tuna.
> One afternoon we saw a dorado fish swimming alongside the boat. Eight days out and we still have the birds with us.

Later

We did motor, just for a titch, galvanised into action by sighting a strange round object bobbing on the sea a short distance from our ship.

Through binoculars, it became a glass-fishing float sometimes seen in fish restaurants—a big one, translucent green with woven netting around it. Couldn't let a goody like that go floating past. No sir. *Banyandah's* straight-six fired up. The mechanical sound alerting those below to something happening. On cue, both boys and their mum pour topside and from the foredeck searched until sighting the object. Then they shared my excitement. Down came the headsail. It hadn't been doing much anyway. And in came the trolling line hanging straight towards the abyss. With a push of the gear lever and a pull of the throttle, we were off in hot pursuit.

Drifting towards the float minutes later, both sons outside the railing, a hand hanging on, the other outstretched, each hoping to be the lucky one to reach the green ball first. Jerome got the prize. He swung a foot out, trapping the ball, then swooped and grabbed hold the netting. Zap! One treasure plucked from the sea.

Judging by the granddaddy gooseneck barnacles, the float had been wandering the world for some time. The side loaded with rubbery elephant trunks with two white claspers at their ends felt far heavier than the spotless upper-side. Other critters lived on that mini-world too. When the float hit the deck, a whole community of crabs jumped ship. About a dozen wee ones and three big brutes with heavy armoured shells and stubby muscular arms dotted with neat rows of hairs. The entire community so small, they would have lain in one boy's hand.

Jason, the sympathetic one grabbed a plastic bucket, dipped it full of seawater, and began easing those freeloaders into it. He coaxed one after another out the small gaps between glass and net. And while we watched this on-board nature lesson, Jude and I realised just how shattering a blow this must be for that microcosm. Geez, before our arrival that bunch of sea buddies had been floating about the world aboard their own tiny adventure machine. The barnacles probably blabbed back and forth, made baby barnacles while days turned into night and back again. The crabs, on the other hand, had the run of the ship. In calm weather, they might have gone topside for a bit of sunbathing or feed on the tasty algae growing on their tiny planet. They might have dared to take short swims out to tasty morsels drifting past. If any sea monsters came out the blue, more than likely they just shrank under the protection of the netting. What a perfect life!

When we came along - swoosh, their entire world went into a spin. Animals seldom protest, so we humans think they don't care, or don't think. But maybe they do.

After Jason collected all the crabs, without thought, he dumped the bucket back into the sea. The crabs were very much alive to be sure, but my God, what a shock. Plopped into such a massive world with their only sanctuary, our ship, speeding away, must have caused a few crab hearts to flutter. Can you imagine? Maybe you've never swum in the middle of the biggest ocean. I have, and it goes on forever, a light blue world without end with no place to hide. The tiniest particle stands out like a billboard flashing, "Here I am! Dinner time!"

Splashed from a bucket into a boundless sea, which way would they go? Surely not down. And what if a hungry fish should happen past? Gulp! We never meant to be cruel. We just wanted the ball. And they would have died on our deck if we hadn't thrown them back. Sometimes doing what we think is right is wrong.

The Right Place at the Wrong Time - Arrival 19 July ~

Start at the Galápagos straddling the equator, head south, travel twenty-five days and twenty-five nights, see not another soul, just sea and sky, catch a few fish, fight a storm, and afterwards drift until an increasing wind brings a black silhouette in the waking hours of a brand new day. Welcome to the navel of the world.

This grassy triangle of volcanic rock has been called the most remote inhabited island in the world. Its nearest population centre lies twenty-three hundred miles across the open ocean in Chile, which has governed Easter Island since annexing it in the 19th century. Twenty-six hundred miles in the other direction is the capital of French Polynesia, Papeete, located on the northwest coast of Tahiti.

As first light shows a stormy sea, we see huge combers pounding a dark red, vertical headland latticed into blocks like giant bricks. Atop that barricade sits a young maiden's breast of yellow and green crowned by a topknot of eucalyptus. This is Poike, the last stronghold of the Long Ears. Welcome to Easter Island - Bienvenidos a la Isla de Pascua - Ia Orana Rapa Nui.

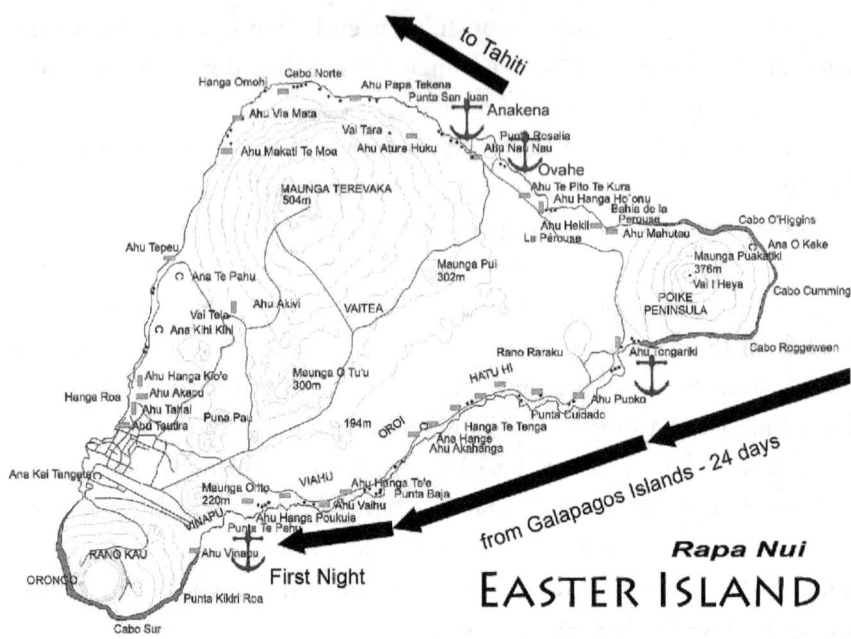

On the horizon, a storm is coming, so we race the gathering wind to shelter behind this mysterious land visited by so few. Hanging on tight we fly past Poike as blasts rush down its treeless slopes sending torrents of froth and spray over our decks. Sheer cliff gives way to a crescent of crumbling rock, the last remains of a long-dead volcano. Standing boldly in the bright morning light is Rano Raraku, the birthplace of the *moai*.

The wind now comes in vicious jabs, so we run close alongside big Southern Ocean combers rumbling high up the rocky shore. And then fly past more worn volcanic cones across a strange open land tilted gently towards the sea so that all can be seen ahead to a collage of pleasing earth colours, browns, reds, and strange heat-fused violets. Next comes a yellow-green grass peppered with small lumps of black rock that God Himself must have sprinkled from the heavens around the silent moai standing guard over Rapa Nui.

The island's bold southern headland appears ahead across a white flecked, windswept sea. It's another dormant volcano. Figures on horseback appear, a dog running alongside. The land dips where the sea breaks less. At last, we see a turquoise bottom. This is Vinapu, an open roadstead, bounded by yet more cliffs in rare earth colours.

To the Navel of the World

"Anchor away," my young son cries out. "Welcome to the island of statues." He laughs.

There's no harbour on this triangular-shaped island ten miles a side; we knew that before setting out. If the wind changes, we run. If a storm attacks, sleep is forsaken, and decisions must be spot-on. But, with our first glimpse, we knew the decision to gamble so much had been a good one. An indescribable aura permeates the air, its presence creating a cone of silence from the storm. If we get no further, our first glimpse will have been worth the long voyage.

But we got much further. Not with any help from the weather. That storm turned out to be just a taste. In our first days, stormy weather forced us to shift six times, forced us to stand watches through black rainy nights, to listen to combers break just behind our ship while violent winds tested our anchors. We lost one.

Getting on the land proved a challenge. But once there, our dreams became a reality. Everyone seemed so kind. Approximately twenty-five hundred Pascuans inhabit the island, dating back to the fourth century when Polynesian voyagers led by Hotu Matu'a arrived. Spanish is spoken. So is Rapa Nui, their dialect of Polynesian. And a little English too.

First European contact came in 1722 when seamen on their holiest Sunday sighted a dot of land from the deck of the Dutch ship, *De Afrikaansche Galei*. Commodore Jacob Roggeveen christened his discovery in honour of the day and wrote in his log; *remarkable primitive tall stone figures caused us to be filled with wonder.*

But discovery did not bring civilisation. Instead, it brought tragedy. Beginning when Roggeveen's landing party inexplicably opened fire on the bewildered islanders, leaving twelve dead and more wounded.

For the next one hundred forty years, ruthless adventurers brought disease, more violence, and death. Then in 1862, Easter Island's strange culture suffered its deathblow. Slavers swooped and carried away about a thousand men to work the fetid guano deposits off the Peruvian coast. Not long after, the Peruvian Government returned the fifteen who survived. Smallpox came with them. The disease ravaged the remaining islanders. When Commodore Roggeveen stepped ashore in 1722, the population stood at approximately four thousand. After the smallpox of 1877, a scant one hundred eleven remained. The last of the kings had perished, and all memory of past greatness lay crushed beneath the island's toppled shrines. Peace did not settle over Rapa Nui until Chile annexed the island in 1888. For a while, the Chilean Navy administered the island and operated an island-wide sheep farm. Its forty thousand sheep provided meat for the inhabitants and wool for export.

After that first storm abated, we shifted *Banyandah* to Hutuiti, the bay under the impressive sight of the silent volcano Rano Raraku. And there, entirely alone we wandered up the extinct volcano to see our cherished *Banyandah* in the blue at its base with a moai standing guard. No matter how many pictures you have seen of the stoic statues, no matter how many accounts you have read of their origin, the first sight of them poses the question of what calamity befell those imposing coastal shrines called *ahu*.

While several moai stand erect, others are on an incline, and many are pushed over on their noses. A few moai remain in the volcanic rock where they were created—noses, foreheads, ears and chins in various forms of completion. Folklore says the statues represent figures of revered ancestors. It also states, lacking wood to carve, artists turned to the abundant workable volcanic rock. Another mystery, many moai once wore cylindrical hats of heavy red stone that had been toppled long ago. Historians say feuds or an epidemic halted all work about three hundred years ago.

As we ambled up Rano Raraku's southwest slope, many monstrous moai are buried to their shoulders, hunched like an army of vanquished colossi. Their grim lips and beetling brows admit defeat. Not by time, not by the elements, perhaps by the death of the culture that sculpted them. They glowered over the island, seemingly across time itself.

From Rano Raraku's volcanic rim, the sea stretched unchanged since creation. Above, a lighter sky kept us company as we slid our hands over the contours of those mysterious creations lying in their birthplace while our souls listened to their secrets. Who? How? Many questions passed through our minds. Such perfection—like the Mona Lisa, not in beauty, but their mood and feeling.

During the middle of our three-week stay, the weather turned balmy, and the sea became flat. Anchored on the north coast in the bay once used by the discoverer La Perouse during his visit of 1786, we strolled upon the vacant land, exploring caves we chanced upon that brought tingling thoughts of discovering hidden treasure. Walking to the cove at

Anakena, which folklore says is the original landing site of Hotu Matu'a, the first king of Rapa Nui, we discovered the remains of a large village. Visible by several stones remaining precisely set in the shape of a sizeable double-ended canoe. They are the foundation of an olden day 'boathouse' built with reeds that still grow in the crater lakes. Also at Anakena is the original statue raised by the Heyerdahl expedition, plus a set of seven others more recently erected with power equipment. Petroglyphs of sinister half-man, half-bird creatures decorate the rock walls of the ahu—the stone temple platform on which the statues stand.

Our second storm struck the day Judith and Jason hiked the ten miles along the island to replenish our supply of food at Hanga Roa, Rapa Nui's only town. The night before had been hot and airless, but with dawn came the touch of a breeze that slowly grew as the day passed. At lunch, a drop of rain fell. After that, the bay became choppy as the wind began blowing onshore.

This was Judith's first trip to town for I'd checked us in accompanied by Jerome. While doing that, we'd met a helpful Pascuan named Orlando Paoa, a few years my senior. We met at the counter of a rustic store where he was speaking a tongue so strange I impulsively blurted out, "What language is that?"

Without hesitation, this solidly built man turned and said, "Why, that's Rapa Nui. When did you arrive?"

Picking up my box of supplies, I replied, "Oh, just this morning." Then bid him a good day.

A few minutes later on the boardwalk alongside the dirt main street, a red and white pickup truck pulled up with my new acquaintance at the wheel. "Can I give you a lift to your boat?" he asked.

"How do you know I came by boat?"

"Planes come only twice a week, the last yesterday."

After that chance encounter, Orlando helped me clear in with the Chilean officials. And next, he assisted with our other purchases and gave us a box of much desired fresh fruits before delivering us across the island, though not before a quick stop at his hotel for a welcoming island drink. His parting words were, "See me again when you need any help." Orlando, a perfect friend to a sea-roving family. So, before Judith departed, I told her where Orlando could be found.

At three that stormy afternoon, with our bay running a nasty sea, Orlando's pickup truck breasted the last hillock from town. We could still land *Little Red*, only because a peninsula of land protected the sandy beach, but the journey across the open swell took careful timing of the oars to miss the wavelets. Orlando, Jude, Jason, and several others piled out the truck and began carting box after box to the shore as I rowed in. Jerome stayed behind, in charge of the ship. Once landed, cameras clicked, and Jude gushed with news of her day. "Oh, what fun. It was fabulous," she ran on, "Super nice people."

From a giant icebox carried by a small army of Pascuans, Orlando poured me a drink of *pisco sour*, and raising a similar glass to his lips, he bid us further safe travels. This man impressed me.

Upon the fine sand of Rainbow Beach looking at the hostile sea, I felt safer with the spike of this new liquor that tasted sweet, yet sour like a daiquiri. It lifted the worry I'd carried most of that day. My features relaxed. The setting must have been right and encouraged by my prompting; Orlando began the story of his life.

Orlando ~

Before they built the airport in the sixties, Easter Island remained a prison for any young blood wanting a look at the rest of the world. A ship arrived only once a year. No other communications were possible. As a lad of fifteen, Orlando yearned for more than containment, and one dark night, he and four others quit their birth land in an open fishing boat. They drifted across the sea in search of other lands, and sixty days later, they found their first landfall. Orlando's story captured my imagination, and in awe, I stood on the coloured sand of Ovahe with my eyes blazing into his. A lasting friendship became fused in those moments.

Upon that landfall, his future dramatically changed and took a very different course. From the tiny Cook Island, where first interned for illegal entry, the authorities put him on the next ship, as fate would dictate, bound for Panama. There he fell in with a group of US servicemen who encouraged him to join the US Air Force. Once enlisted, he gained higher education while serving twenty years rising in rank. Here is fate's second twist—when NASA needed a Pacific Ocean tracking station for the Gemini space program, they shipped Orlando home to help build the Easter Island Airport so that NASA could establish a tracking station on his island. Now Orlando owns one of Rapa Nui's finer hotels. Concluding his tale, Orlando called over a tall young man with thick black hair. I meet Benjamin, one of his sons, a handsome twenty-three-year-old man.

Benjamin seated centre

Looking over my shoulder, Orlando told me something I already knew. "Jack, a storm is coming. You will have to move your ship."

Thinking of my worrisome day, I smiled. "Yeah. As soon as we get these supplies on board, we'll be away."

Silent for a moment, Orlando continued looking out to sea then abruptly spoke. "Why don't we trade sons for the night, my one for your two? Yours can come home with me, have a shower, and watch television. My son can experience a night at sea."

How could I refuse such a kind man? I didn't think the storm would be fierce.

I turned and asked, "Benjamin, do you get seasick?"

A shake of his jet-black curls was his reply, so I said, "Okay, let's load up. I'll bring Jerome ashore."

Half an hour later, the transfer complete, I'm swearing and cursing. Our anchor jammed in that confounded Easter Island rock kept *Banyandah* rolling violently—Benjamin limp and spewing all over my boat.

When finally away, *Banyandah* streaked across La Perouse Bay with the Three Crosses atop Poike our landmark ahead. Once they were close aboard, we roared past that red wall of gigantic bricks, white surf flying high and the sea running freely across our decks. Quickly again at Tongoriki, the bay at the base of Rano Raraku, but this time much further out for the swell had built and broke in deadly white lines across the entrance to the shallow bay.

In gathering dusk, we anchored deep, letting fathoms of line out after buoying our anchor. With no-where else to hide, our existence became a screeching windblown night of worry. Each blast topped the last, sending clouds racing across the full moon which made the night alternate between Stygian blackness and ghoulish light showing glimpses of a volcano above a madhouse of white danger. Waves tumbled, making the ocean glow as if drowning sailors danced upon windblown spume in the cacophony of their screeches. As the angry sea thundered past, our anchor rope protested like a creature torn between colossal forces making sleep impossible. Instead, we worried if our line should break? Regaining land might take days, if ever.

Daylight brought a white world gone crazy. Through storm spray, it surprised me to see land still before us, and the vague shape of a moai looking back. Inured by years at sea, and memories of screeching wind and angry seas, we got on with daily life. But bedridden Benji became a worry. He could not drink nor eat.

The peak of the storm passed with first light, and by late afternoon, although still blowing a full gale, a small boat put out from the shore. Pitching bows high, a familiar figure came riding the white waves like a rodeo star—Orlando, a broad grin lighting his face.

"The boys are okay." He had to yell across the small gap after the open craft containing two others circled astern and ploughed back alongside. "I'll keep them safe until this blows out."

Hearing his father's voice, Benji jumped out the forward cabin bunk and ran until sighting his father, when, quick as a wink, he leapt into the sea and swam for their craft. Orlando, with an even greater smile lighting the dull day, waved hugely over his head before they turned to smash through head seas back to their land. Jude and I, now alone, prayed for their safety while watching their single outboard struggle.

From that day on, we became a regular in the Paoa house; besides showers, lunches, shopping excursions, and tours of the island, we also got together for stories of folklore. Nothing was too much, and our friendship, knowing a time limit existed, grew with rapid delight.

When quiet days returned, we ventured further from our home under the guidance of Orlando, who took great pride in showing us several Rapa Nui cultural sites. One day as we bumped along a rough track in his pickup truck, the boys hanging on dearly in the tray, he told us that there were hundreds of statues and ceremonial platforms. That day he wanted to take us to Ana Kai Tangata, known as the cave of cannibals. Mentioning that oral legends talk of cannibalism by the champion clan of the Tangata Manu, but he thought them hogwash. His people were not cannibals; this was a cave of learning.

Breasting a hill overlooking the sea near the airport runway, we jumped out to follow him to the sea edge and following his gaze saw a volcanic opening next to foaming breakers just above the high tide line that allowed easy access.

The boys were excited, as were Judith and I, so we wasted no time in scrambling along a path to the opening, which looked about five metres high and twice that in width. Looking in, amazement lit our faces because the cave went in a long way.

Inside we found impressive acoustics. The boys' echoes rebounded back and forth off the lava walls, as did Orlando's booming voice explaining that the name of the cave could mean many things.

"*Ana*, of course, is cave. *Tangata* means man. But *Kai* can mean eat, gather or tell. There's no proof of cannibalism known on Easter Island, so I prefer *Cave of Learning*, especially as there are such outstanding acoustics and paintings."

Moving to the inner vault where he could just stand erect, he said, "Come over here."

Gathering about him, we saw a cave painting in red, white, and black, which appeared to be birds.

"Manutara," he said with reverence, "the good luck bird."

Wondering how old the cave painting might be, Orlando began to explain how, in the 16th century, the Birdman cult displaced the worship of the moai, the stone statues, when food became scarce, and the clans fought each other. Orlando told us that the competition to decide Tangata Manu, the Birdman, was a peaceful way of settling who should have the rights to the annual harvest of sea bird's eggs.

"You need to visit Rano Kao and see the cult village of Orongo. Let me organise my guide to take you there tomorrow."

Next day, Christian picked us up in the truck and took us to the island's southern tip. On the way, he told us that the extinct volcano Rano Kao is not known for giant stone statues, as are the other volcanoes, but rather for its spectacular beauty.

After walking the *Te Ara O Te Ao* trail, not knowing what to expect upon reaching the top, the large caldera overwhelmed us. Inside, the accumulation of rainwater had formed a lagoon more than a kilometre in diameter. Looking as if Monet had painted a collage of green splattered with glistening blue lakes lined with reeds, we were both excited and impressed. Further enchantment came when looking upon the crater's green and brown-streaked walls, and we saw hawks ride the thermals in great circles. Following them across the crater, the bird cult ruins could be seen enjoying a magnificent location above the lagoon lying two hundred metres below the rim.

"Come," Christian beckoned. "Let's examine the ceremonial houses." Saying that, Christian led us around the rim of Easter Island's mightiest extinct volcano to the deserted village of Orongo. There the boys exclaimed in amazement when seeing stones beautifully adorned with birdmen petroglyphs and other strange creatures.

The fifty-three squat houses standing on the brink of a drop off commanding the open sea were not the common *hare vaka* (boat houses) constructed from lightweight volcanic stone filled with air pockets. Instead, they were built entirely out of *kehu,* a heavy flat stone that helped the houses survive the strong winds at the top of the volcano. We stood alongside them on the knife-edge peering over a cerulean sea, and listened to tales of rongorongo, a system of glyphs as mysterious as the statues, and heard details of the competition that determines the Birdman.

Christian said the name suggested half-man half-bird, representing the living deity the isolated population needed, reminding us that on an island without large mammals or reptiles, birds provided protein in meat and eggs. That led to a belief that birds held a mystical relationship with gods, especially the seabirds that united the earth, sea, and sky. This became paramount in the 15th century when food ran short, and the birds of Easter Island became significant for ritual, spiritual, and economic reasons.

Calling our attention to the petroglyphs, Christian told us that the bird chosen for the Birdman emblem is the frigate bird, one of the great predators of the Pacific and capable of flying vast distances.

Christian started telling us how the islanders had practised a curious religious rite centred upon the eggs of the sooty tern. As we listened, we could visualise the chiefs of the most influential clans and their families moving into these large communal houses that overlook the three islets of Motu Kao Kao (sharp island), Motu Iti (small island) and Motu Nui (large island) the nesting place of migratory sooty terns.

Each chief appointed one, sometimes two *hopu*, loosely meaning aid or helper, to descend the cliffs and swim to the farthest and largest island, Motu Nui, to await the terns and hopefully return with the first egg. The island of Motu Nui lays a thousand metres from the cliffs. That made the swim very dangerous. Sharks attacked hopu, some drowned, while others fell from the cliffs. Those that completed the swim settled in caves to wait for the first egg to be laid. During this wait, the chiefs and the rest of the population held ritual dances and prayer ceremonies at the stone village of Orongo. These often lasted weeks.

Once the first egg was collected, the finder climbed to the highest point on Motu Nui and called out to his benefactor, telling him, "Go shave your head, you have the egg!" Hearing this, the unsuccessful hopu collectively swam back to the main island while the egg-finder remained on Motu Nui, fasting until his benefactor had shaved his head before putting on a wig of human hair, and was painted with the ritual colours of red and white.

Only after that did the *hopu manu* swim back, doing this with the egg secured inside a reed basket tied to his forehead. On reaching land, he had to climb the steep, rocky cliff and, if he did not fall, present the egg to his patron who the priest then declared Tangata Manu. The new

Birdman was entitled to gifts of food and other tributes, including his clan having sole rights to collect that season's harvest of wild bird eggs and fledglings from Motu Nui.

Although the Birdman cult remained in practice until Christian missionaries arrived in the 1860s, the flag of Easter Island included the Birdman emblem until 1888.

As the beautiful weather lingered, we became saturated with island lore, but the worry of new storms remained topmost in my thoughts. Rapa Nui is a difficult, dangerous location. Why push our luck I kept thinking until yielding to my uneasiness when I mentioned departure. Once spoken, the move became definite and our efforts turned to re-provisioning. Here again, our island friend came to our aid. His truck made many trips across the bumpy dirt track carrying supplies and boxes of his garden's produce. When I mentioned needing water, the next day he arrived with drums of sweet rainwater. I mentioned cooking gas, and like a magician, two full cylinders showed up on our beach. We decanted gas from his cylinder by standing his on the dry-stone wall with our bottles on the ground. Now Jude could make bread whenever she liked.

We took time off during these forays for a fun, island-style, fish barbeque organised naturally by Orlando. In a gala affair at Ovahe with the colourful Rainbow Beach surrounded by cliffs of reddish volcanic origin before us, we sat upon rocks overlooking the statues with plates of island fare balanced upon our knees. Beside me, the man who had made our visit so complete. In my happy reverie, distant sounds of the faraway brought thoughts of Orlando's long-ago sea adventure.

This small beach that is more a cove of turquoise with fine pink sand a mixture of volcanic slag and eroded white coral was perfect for dreaming.

Turning to him, I said, "Orlando, come with us."

Looking deeply into his eyes, he quietly nodded as I added, "You should join *Banyandah* for the sail to Tahiti."

Excitement blossomed in his grey eyes, but the starburst soon dwindled and died. I guess he hadn't the freedom to say yes. His business demanded his daily presence.

With a touch of regret, he said "I cannot. But why not take Benji?"

His words brought back a vision of Benji doubled over and retching, so I nodded then slowing shook my head before replying that we'd not see land for over twenty days. Then with a gasp, I added if Benji thought he could manage, we'd welcome him aboard *Banyandah*.

Orlando called his son. He was intelligent like his father, so I described best I could the hardships of such a voyage, which he considered for a moment, then to my great surprise, he accepted.

"Why?" I asked. "You get seasick."

Looking me straight in the face, with great maturity, he said the words I will never forget. "It is an opportunity I may never have again. So I must."

Only, it wasn't that easy. Although the island population might have been excited, even envious, officials barred our way. Only Chilean officials can grant an exit visa to Pascuans, and Chilean officialdom rates alongside the most officious in the world. Benji also needed a passport. For several days, I delayed departure while Orlando battled with Chilean immigration. He made telephone calls overseas, elicited favours from friends, bullied his way through red tape until finally receiving the permission for his son to sail with us.

That prompted a hastily arranged grand finale barbecue in front of *Banyandah* at Anakena, the cradle of Rapa Nui history and culture. During the afternoon before this, the *Four J's* walked across the grass plains to Rano Raraku to say goodbye to our rock friends who have looked over their island for centuries.

Along the shores and around the base of the volcano, the moai stand stoically facing inland. Long faces set in remorse. Had they watched their island wither and die? Had they endured the sad helplessness of being unable to alter the outcome after the islanders' wanton behaviour damaged the island's resources beyond repair?

Passing my hand over the smooth moai brought thoughts of the men who created the statutes of these deified ancestors, and a weird empathy crept inside me. Perhaps the island spirits infiltrated my soul for I felt their remorse. Our journey around the world had shown a similar transformation underway that seemed as resistant to alter course. From that moment, I would be forever stricken by this island's primitive connection with Earth.

Alas, like a whirlwind, fast and exciting came our barbecue with plenty of new friends, many laughs, more stories, a promised reunion.

This ended with the coming twilight when we made our final goodbyes. Tears flowed as if we were leaving our home.

To a chorus of Rapa Nui songs, Jason and Jerome rowed us out to *Banyandah* with Benji in the bow strumming his ukulele. Something we were to hear a lot more while sailing to Tahiti.

For a final time, the anchor rose from the rock bottom of Rapa Nui. The boys hoisted sail, and on a kind breeze, *Banyandah* edged towards a cloud-scattered horizon rapidly filling with gold. And like a play coming to an end, daylight dwindled, taking the island from our sight as we headed towards our next adventure.

Exclaimed in amazement seeing stones beautifully adorned with birdmen petroglyphs and other strange creatures.

To the Navel of the World

Tales of rongorongo, a system of glyphs as mysterious as the statues.
Carved on a piece of *Banyandah's* trim by Benji while sailing on our voyage to Tahiti.

Reflections in a Sailor's Eyes

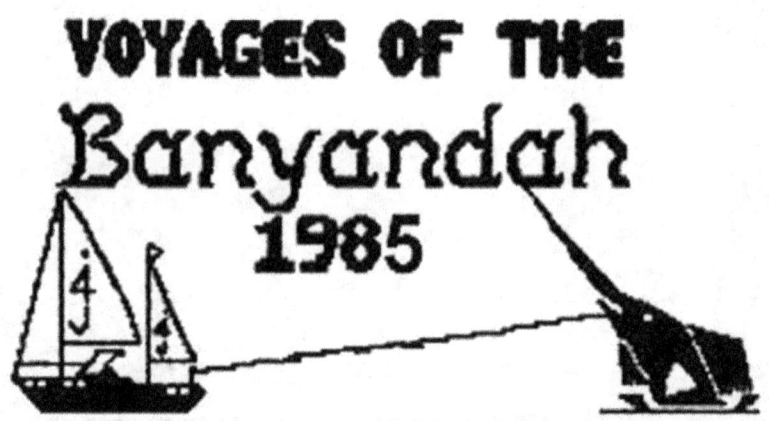

Computer art hand coded by Jason and Jerome

Mauke Island in the vast South Pacific

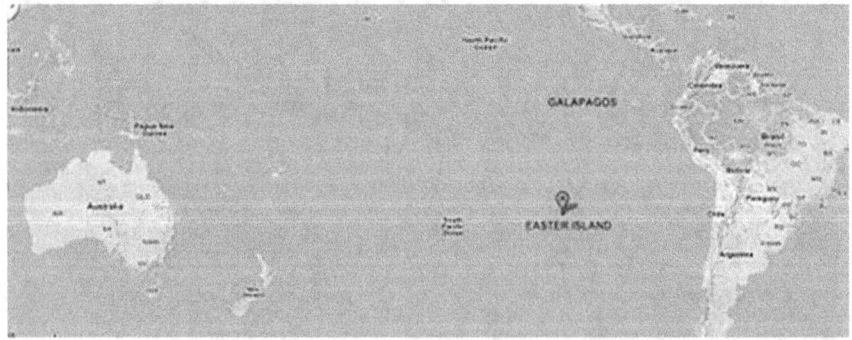

THE ONE THAT GOT AWAY

by Cap'n Jack in 1985, on board *Banyandah*, Pacific Ocean

Hooked a monster fish yesterday, and gosh, do I hurt. On my right hand, the fishing line burnt a grey-white path through layers of skin, while on the soft underside of my arm an angry welt rises like a crimson snake. They are painful injuries, but I'll not complain because they remind me of a battle between man and beast, and keep alive the vision of a beautiful creature.

As with many of our adventures in Nature's world, this episode came upon us quite suddenly. One moment we were pleasantly sailing through an empty blue world of sunshine and sea. The next, the whole ship erupted with running kids and parents, each yelling, gesticulating, colliding with the other, while the cause of this slapstick madness rushed after us like a dark sinister torpedo connected to our ship by what looked an overly-stretched wire.

Just before this adventure began, under far more miserable conditions, we had sighted then passed Mauke Island, the most eastern of the Cook Isles. Until spotting that bit of land, dark clouds and rain had kept us below in an airless cabin for five hundred miles. Adding to our misery, we hadn't landed a fish even though we'd towed one of Jerome's choicest lures for four days and four nights. But sighting that grey smudge of land on the windward horizon changed all of that. As if that island had been a gateway to better times, sailing past it brought an immediate clearing that turned the sea turquoise while the clouds became fleecy white. And even though we had just eaten lunch, the prospect of more tinned food conjured up thoughts of catching a fish supper. So while the boys and Jude teased the trolling line hoping for a strike, I had snuggled into a quiet corner to fashion a new lure from the silver bladder of a spent wine cask. I slit it to form numerous tentacles then wrapped three turns around a homemade head made from a sinker and seized it on tight using light thread. Jiggled in the sunshine, if I were a fish, I'd not be able to resist it.

Mauke was two hours astern when my lure joined Jerome's. Now two little beauties danced a welcome to hungry fish, their flashy skirts cleverly hiding sharp double hooks.

"FISH!" The word roared out my mouth the moment I saw the line stretched taut in our wake.

"It's a big one." I warned, pulling Jerome away after he'd come running aft with his small hands outstretched to grab the line. He'd been ready to pit his young muscles against the power of that beast. Holding his shoulders, my eye followed the trolling line into the dark blue of deep sea. Nothing could be seen of our monster. Nothing until its body was backlit by the low afternoon sun through a clear blue mid-ocean swell. Its dark shadow indicating it was bigger than me.

"Sweet Jesus," I murmured. Then louder so the whole family could hear, "It must be a giant tuna or..." I stammered unable to put a name to the beast. Ordering the boys to clear the other line, a shiver of fear raced up my arms as I felt Jude rush up behind me. While the boys furiously hauled in the slack line, forming an untidy heap on the deck, she asked me, "What is it? What kind of fish grows so big?"

I knew lots of sea creatures grew that big: Sharks, tuna, marlin, sailfish. Of the lot, the marlin was the big baddy, the real heavy weight fighter. And the shadow I'd glimpsed of powerful shoulders, sleek body running back to a crescent shaped tail, had looked a lot like that brute.

Banyandah, her main and headsail still set, was coursing through the mild afternoon sea as I tested the tautness of the line with one hand. The line ran direct, man to beast, and like a telegraph wire bringing a message, a feeling of the upcoming battle sprang to mind. Suddenly, memories of other battles brought images of pain, and I remembered tempers flaring, hands being cut, and how once I'd nearly been dragged off the boat.

"Maybe he'll throw the hook." Jude suggested when she saw pain crease my face.

"Christ, I hope so." I snapped, "I just want my line back."

On *Banyandah*, we didn't have any of those expensive Penn Reels found on the big game fishing boats. Our gear was simple. Fifty meters of braided nylon cord like that used on venetian blinds runs to a hefty swivel, where it changed to one hundred kilogram mono-filament for another fifty meters, then wire trace. It was all heavy duty stuff. We wanted to catch fish, not play with them, or lose gear. But without rods and reels, the fish had to be hauled in by hand. Jerome and his older brother Jason pulled in medium sized fish up to ten kilos. After that, they were mine. Some were a battle. The big ones, dangerous. We once hooked a powerhouse yellow fin tuna bigger than me on a delivery voyage crossing the Indian Ocean, and for more than an hour, I wrestled that brute, hauling line in, only to be forced to let it out when he made a run for it. That one really tore up my hands.

Gripping the cord connecting this monster to my ship, I knew I wouldn't go through that again. One choice was to do nothing and hope the beast freed itself. But sharks home in on stranded animals. Besides, it might drown. That may sound strange, but if its mouth was held open, which could happen if hooked in its lower jaw, water would be forced into its stomach. Smaller fish had come on board so full their bellies had burst. The alternative was to haul in line every time it broke surface, every time it relented its awesome force. Maybe then I could cut it free at the hook.

In a voice pitched high by tension, I told the kids to keep clear. "I'm going to try'n haul him close enough to cut the trace. You Jerome, run for the side cutters. And get a knife too." I called after he sped for the tool cabinet in the aft cabin.

Putting a hand on Jason's shoulder, I looked into his soft puppy eyes. "Son, make sure the free line stays away from me. Understand? If it runs, I may have to let go. And please, for God's sake, be careful. Don't let it get caught up in your arms." His eyes widened hearing my last remark so I pulled him into an embrace. "Just do as I say and you'll be all right," I lovingly whispered into his ear before asking if he was ready. With a nod, my oldest broke our embrace, but not sure of where to stand, he fluttered around like a fly in a tizzy. Taking a deep breath, I turned aft to the endless sea and took up the strain, being surprised by how easy the line came in. Quickly I hauled while Jason leapt in and out, delicately pulling the tangles away from my person while a pile of wet cord built up in mere seconds. Half came in easily, but then, as if that fish had decided that was as far as he'd go, he ground me to a halt. His powerful thrusts moved the line to our side, cutting the sea like a stretched wire cuts cheese. Using every ounce of my strength I held him although his tugs for freedom stretched me far out over the railing.

Intimately connected, I felt his will to live. In jerks, it travelled to my hands, up my arms, through my whole body. Half of me was filled with blood lust where kill craze reigned supreme. My other half prayed the hooks would straighten and the beast would burst free.

For a time we held each other in check, our spirits connected. He'd jerk, I'd resist, and in the standoff my mind floated free. Old feelings surfaced. In flash after flash, I relived scenes from other big battles, and again the lust to conquer rose within me. From back in the deep reaches, I heard the profane shouts my kill craze had brought out, and once again, I saw a huge creature struggle for his last moments of dear life. I saw the blood, the snapping jaw, its round eye losing lustre.

I must have relaxed my hold. Or maybe my soft feelings had crept down the line because all at once this monster gave an enormous jerk and the white braid tore from my grip. Its heat burned as it ran through my hand and I knew that I'd have to triple my grip or it'd tear my hand open. Dropping the line, I pushed Jason clear of the unwinding pile and yelled, "Get back! He's running!" That line flew out as if connected to an arrow shot across the sea. Then in an eye blink, it was bowstring tight again.

Stopped in flight, the beast must have been wrenched around with a force I can only imagine. A force doubled by *Banyandah's* swiftly sailing across the mild sea. The whiplash would have killed any man. But as it snapped taut, the line gave my inner arm a solid slap. Blood would rise where it hit.

Grimacing in pain, I turned to my family. "It's no use. I can't hold him. I haven't the strength."

"Use the winch, dad." Jerome's voice was trembling, excited by the action. Danger was a part of our life and we operated under its threat daily. But to free the beast using the winch would require their help, therefore I was worried my boys could be injured or maimed.

Unsure of what to do, I reluctantly agreed. "Okay, we'll give that a try. But we'll need to take the line outside the hand railing." Then I warned them. "Here's where someone can lose a hand or finger, so we must be careful."

As I took hold of the line, I felt the salt bite and noticed for the first time the grey-white grooves in my fingers. There'd be time for looking after them later, so right then I put the pain in a closed box and pulled in some slack for the boys to work with. Around me while restrained the line, two lads excited by hooking one of the world's biggest fish, pushed each other and fumbled the line, arguing who should do what until I snapped.

"Stop it! Shut your mouths, both of you." Panting, I stopped to stare them down. "You call that team work. Jerome, get that line through the gate….. No! Under the chain or it'll be cut in a flash. Jason, get it on the winch. A single wrap, man. Or it'll roll over itself and get jammed."

With the line running from the beast, up the side of our vessel, around a smooth stainless steel stanchion to the winch we used to crank in the headsails, I ordered the kids to stand back. "I'll not have either of you hurt. Just take in the slack as I haul him in."

Blood pounded through my veins as I turned to face our embattled victim who chose that moment to make a spectacular leap, his magnificent form clearing the sea. Sunshine shone on his silvery sides, highlighting mauve markings that sparkled with droplets from the sea. His bill pointed skywards, the line direct to my hands while his eye bore straight into mine.

He looked frightened. Like a harmless creature trapped in a battle for life by his own instinctive nature. In that instant the heat vanished from my heart. In a strange flash of recognition, I saw the sad eyes of my oldest son on his face. Saw in his very posture the look of my sons when they call for help. All blood lust left me and all I wanted was to free this young thing so that once again he could freely wander his world as I and my loved ones wandered ours.

Gently, and slowly because this young beast still easily outmatched our strength, we pulled him closer to the boat using the winch. When pulled close enough for him to recognise its underwater shape, he danced once again on his sickle shaped tail. But he could not break free. After that leap, he gave up, lying over on his side, the sweeping arc of his huge pectoral fin standing erect as if a conning tower on a futuristic Jules Verne craft.

Not fighting one bit, he came in until the double prong hook could be seen implanted in the middle of his upper bill. Good, not in his gills. That would have been fatal. Nor swallowed into his gut. That too would have caused death.

Pulled up to the boat he proved quite docile. Looking at him eye to eye told me why. He was trembling with fear like a frightened puppy being pulled up to an ungodly monster. He thought his life was about to end. And so it might if another had hooked him.

Jerome snatched at the wire trace with our boat hook then brought the creature alongside. Moving with speed, I reached through the railing as close as I dare while being cautious of his bill that was the length of my arm and sharp like a dagger. Not wanting to chance an injury, one eye was on that weapon when I slid the side cutters down the wire. Reaching as far as I could, I silently wished him well then closed my grip. Hardly any pressure had bore when the wire snapped and our young monster slid astern while *Banyandah* continued gliding through the sea unaware that a great adventure had just ended.

Jude, Jason, and Jerome gathered around me to watch the fellow take off with his life. For a few brief seconds, he remained lifeless on his side in our wake. Then he shook his frame in a powerful thrust, sea splashing into the air. And with a last glimpse of silver, mauve, and black, he was gone.

"Did you see that?" Shouted Jason, eyes wide, astonished.

"Poor fellow, do think he'll get that hook out of his mouth?" Jude asked, her concern prompting me to slip my good arm around her.

As the ring of disturbed water merged with the sea, I answered. "Sure babe, it'll dissolve and he'll have no problems from now on."

RHUMB LINES AROUND AUSTRALIA

Scudding clouds clip The Hazards of Tasmania's Wineglass Bay, the same pink granite mountains that French explorer Freycinet sailed from in 1802. Cold wetness is falling and the sea ahead foams white to an open horizon. It calls to our spirits to run free, to close the last link and complete the circle around earth's largest inhabited island. Every link has needed strength and courage, each has been as different as the colours in a rainbow.

To not lose the weather edge, we must commit to the south wind's fury to sail north, knowing we'll be alone at sea, not for hours, but days exceeding a week. Why is it we gamble our lives trekking the wild places? Why do we sally forth without thought of assistance, with few comforts, and fewer companions?

We go where there are no rules, except nature's — survive. No marked lanes. No stop lights. Earth and her creatures will provide wonder and knowledge, adventure and entertainment. As if wandering through the Garden of Eden, they reveal mysteries beyond wisdom and bring knowledge by simply observing life.

In 1803 Captain Mathew Flinders RN became the first to circumnavigate the fifth continent, producing a map of remarkable accuracy on which for the first time the name "Australia" was provocatively inscribed. Mathew Flinders would have found Terra Australis little changed from when man first wandered its vastness, but his map would dramatically change that.

A bit more than two centuries later, Judith and I set out to circumnavigate the great continent of Australia to visit areas we'd not seen before and to compare images from past adventures with the present. We journeyed 9,000 nm over 27 months through three climatic zones, witnessing a myriad collection of life. Our culture tends to dominate the wild kingdom, taking what's wanted and needed, leaving less for the other creatures. Jude and I wonder if that's right. So we search to witness Man's effect.

Leaving our home port of Ballina and taking the familiar trades north, we hardly stopped until Darwin. Soon after we discovered a phenomenon scientists have yet to explain. Rock art without pigment; flowing figures etched in stone. Our best minds claim this is the planet's first art. Once we found one, our mission became to discover others, no matter how remote. We sailed dangerous waters, tramped hostile lands, cataloguing many finds.

Entering the Berkeley River on the west side of Joseph Bonaparte Gulf is quite dangerous. A massive sand bar changing every wet season obstructs it. Best approach is close behind Reveley Island, which helps block the gulf's swell. When close, I called on VHF requesting any vessel inside to relay their GPS entry waypoints and was rewarded when the charter ship *True North* came back with a torturous route that got us within cooee when, "Phut" — our laptop ran out of power. Oops, back to eyeball navigation. Once in, mid-river affords plenty of depth. We parked at the confluence with Casuarina Creek, launched *Little Red*, mounted the outboard, loaded her with drinking water, sounding line, and handheld GPS and then set off to survey the creek.

At first we didn't think *Banyandah* could navigate such a narrow waterway. The low tide had exposed a mere boat length between mud banks. But to our surprise there'd be enough water at half tide to float her 1.8 m draught. Jude commented that it might be okay for a day visit, but difficult to anchor there overnight. But my sailor's eye had already found strong points to secure our ship between island and waterfall, so we gave it a go on the next morning's rising tide.

From rock ledges above the Casuarina Creek waterfall, Bradshaw rock art overlooks tranquil pools. In mulberry red on yellow rock, hunters held boomerangs and spears with their prey around them. Intrigued, and learning to look for flat rock faces protected from the elements, we soon discovered several others that are a shutterbug's delight. Before taking any photographs, we studied every detail to better understand what the artists meant. After thousands of years, many had lost clarity by natural oxidation, changing the stone from straw to deepening reds that conceals the artwork. But we clearly saw a proud race depicted with armlets, fancy hairdos, in ceremonial headdress and grass skirts, and the animals they hunted: goannas, kangaroos, and turtles.

First recorded in 1891 by Joseph Bradshaw who, after becoming lost in the northwest while looking for new grazing lands, sketched in his journal what have become known as the Bradshaw Paintings. According to legend, they were made by birds pecking the rock until their beaks bled, and then they created these fine paintings by using a tail feather and their own blood. But the only known fact is that no pigment remains, making it impossible to carbon date. Whatever was used is locked into the rock, impervious to the elements. The dating of this rare art is based on a 1996 discovery by Mr Grahame Walsh of a fossilised mud wasp's nest partly covering a painting. Scientists, using a new technique, determined that wasp nest to be more than 17,500 years old. While some experts claim 40,000 years, for sure it's at least four to five times the age of classic Egyptian art. Hence the mystery surrounding who, or what, created it.

There is a heap of rock art along the Kimberley coast, both Bradshaw and aboriginal. At Raft Point, amazing red rock turrets tower above the sea that contain well preserved displays of Wandjina art telling the story of their Kaiara God trapping cod at the spiritual place of Langgi where we'd visited a few days before. This area also had a great number of humpback whales tail flapping, pec slapping, and breaching around our ship. One old bull swam straight at us, giving us the willies. Shaky hands clutched the video while that beast charged to within metres. Then he dove, showering us with his wet breath.

Just a bit further west, be very careful around King Sound. Tidal streams exceeding 12 knots could easily destroy your boat. Whole islands rise out the sea, so careful planning is essential. In fact, travelling anywhere in the Kimberley requires diligence and care. It is very isolated and turbid water hides dangers, plus crocs much larger than a dinghy abound, and there is often little wind, so patience and an easily driven vessel are helpful. On the positive side, there are scads of anchorages and tons of adventures and some of the most beautiful scenery found anywhere. You simply must drive your vessel down either the Berkeley or King George River red rock gorges to truly know boating heaven.

One hundred and seventy nautical miles offshore from Broome lay Rowley Shoals, a nature lover's paradise untouched except by global warming. We braved the dangerous narrow entry into Clarke Lagoon to witness red-billed tropic birds breeding on Bedwell Island.

Keeping our distance, we beheld gorgeous fluffy chicks under mother's wings, right through to marbled adolescents attempting first flight. In the pristine waters multitudes of fish far beyond beauty brought joyous hours viewing while little cleaner fish nipped the hairs on our legs then dashed off through vibrant living corals reminiscent of the Great Barrier Reef when we first started cruising. Pity, the GBR is now bleached dead white in places.

WA's summer headwinds proved a tough battle that forced other yachts to turn back. They missed a coast of friendly folk filled with history, enticing us to spend weeks at Dampier, Montebello Isles, Carnarvon, Shark Bay, Albrohos, Fremantle and Geographe Bay. But to our great dismay, we also witnessed the new coming. Oil fields, gas fields, iron-ore mines, large ships plying the seas and road trains raising dust storms on what used to be wild kingdom. That had us wondering, will Man never stop taking over the Earth?

Offshore from Dampier, the Montebello Islands, site of three atomic bomb tests, were thought not too radioactive to stop us visiting. Landing on a wide smile of warm sand, we nervously cringed when a rusty sign warned visitors not to stay ashore longer than an hour. Containing a bouquet of low isles upon a taut canvas of sapphire, care is required because the lagoon is mostly shallow, so we mostly moved on a rising tide. After enjoying giant crayfish that probably would have glowed in the night, we hitched our sails to a rare northerly, taking them to Northwest Cape, where we unwillingly did battle with a 100 kg sailfish. In a three-hour tussle, our best lure was retrieved and the beast set free. But instead of being rewarded for our kindness, those heartless south winds returned, driving our lee rail under for four wet days and nights. Carnarvon Sailing Club eased our bruises with Friday happy-hour barbecues. Then on weekends, Murray from *Salad Days* loaned us his Ute to run our errands and tour the desiccated hinterland.

Shark Bay, what can we say? Scenic beauty, fascinating history, magnificent wildlife, calm water and isolation; everything a cruising yachtsman desires. Except the sea grass, which clogged our anchor triple-fast. The weather allowed us to park off the red sands of Cape Peron to watch the dolphins give preening cormorants a fright. We have footage of them charging the birds up onto the beach. Every morning at famous Monkey Mia, families of dolphins swam past us for a free feed at the beach. And from the museum on the shore we learnt heaps about our marine brothers. Dirk Hartog Island is no longer a working sheep farm; it's now a low-key resort on a world-heritage island. But, with permission, it's still possible to see 100-year-old shearing sheds, shifting dunes equalling the Sahara, and massive schools of sharks and shovelnose guitarfish basking in the warm shallow waters. It took another overnight pounding to reach Geraldton, which we'd visit again just to go back to the Maritime Museum's superb display of salvaged Dutch ship remnants. We'd skip the rest to spend more time in the Houtman Abrolhos. Plenty of wrecks there and history enough to whet the dullest imagination; good anchorages too and fairly all right snorkelling, although the water's getting a tad cold for bare-skin-diving. Curious seals attest to that.

From there, direct to Rottnest, playground for West Australia's rich — and the rest of us. Where in, "summertime, the living is easy . . . " And there's fantastically clear water, a zillion boats and an island bus costing little to hop on and off. This lovely holiday island was first sighted by Dutch navigator Vlamingh on the last day of 1696. A few days later, Willem rowed 18 km up a waterway, which he named Swan River.

In 1978, *Banyandah* first sailed into Fremantle from Sri Lanka. Arriving there this time completed her Aussie circumnavigation — albeit with a 30-year break. And the Fremantle Sailing Club applauded her efforts with a showcase berth where friends and peers stopped to visit.

Fremantle is jumping since the America's Cup. There are now thousands of marina berths, all full, and new seaside flats. But it has retained the lovely old buildings, and there are free buses to scores of eateries, museums and the Fremantle Market. A month was hardly enough. But our sights were set on the untouched land of southwest Tasmania.

Having crossed the Bight once in mid-winter we knew storm cells can generate enormously powerful waves higher than many buildings. A strong gale while rounding Cape Leeuwin reminded us of that. In Albany, we carefully checked and repacked our safety gear before committing to the long haul across the Bight. Albany's Emu Point Slipway has to be the friendliest, best protected place to prepare a vessel for the Southern Ocean. Thanks, Darren, for your superb help.

We've written about our adventures on that crossing in "Moonlight across the Southern Ocean," noting that punching south through the high pressure cell dominant in summer to find the westerlies proved much wiser than slogging against the prevailing east winds blowing along the coast.

Reaching Tasmania's wild west coast, we slipped into Macquarie Harbour through narrow Hell's Gate, named by 19th-century convicts entering the world's harshest prison. Manoeuvring past dangerous eddies and currents, we entered a world filled with nature's beauty and man's history. Using Strahan as our base, we received plenty of assistance from Trevor and Megs, who run the charter yacht *Stormbreaker*. Their friendship, and Trevor's superb hand-drawn chart, made it possible to explore every corner of Macquarie Harbour and take our sailing home high up the Gordon River to walk ancient forests and live among its wild creatures. In contrast, while at Strahan, our anchor chain became denuded of its protective galvanised coating; eaten by contaminants from past copper mines.

An overnight sail south, Nature is different at Port Davey, a world-heritage national park nearly untouched since creation. Battered by southern storms, white granite pushes up through a mosaic of green and gold button grass that looks like a net holding the rock from bursting skywards. Here the Needwonnee people lived in harmony with the planet for 30,000 years. At the far end of Stephens Bay is a wave of sand several stories high, clean and pure except where a tea-stained trickle has cut a channel that discolours it. Approaching it, my boots crunched upon shells and looking over the drifts, I noticed the wind had blown the dune not smooth, but bumpy as if infected with smallpox.

Littering the dune sides were saucer-shaped abalone among turban spirals, along with flat scallops and bivalves. Skirting this area with the greatest respect, we soon noticed both small and large bones among the shells, possibly those of swans from nearby Hannants Inlet, wallabies from the moor lands, seals and mutton bird from nearby islands. The sand extends inland, flooding among a stand of trees in a slight hollow. The trickle of water we first noticed weaves through this and standing upon a slight rise, the ancient homestead of the Needwonne people came into focus.

While at Port Davey, I read Deny King's life story to Judith and learnt that tin had been discovered near Point Eric in 1891; alluvial tin ideally suited to recovery with pick and shovel that Deny King's father, Charles, mined after the 1930s world depression had left him unemployed. Deny went to help his father after World War II and "liked the southwest straightaway. The beautiful scenery, the way the mountains slope down to the sea and the wildness of it all." Charles mined tin there for 21 years, and Deny, who first lived with his father at Cox Bight on the south coast then alongside the inlet at Melaleuca, for a total of 50 years. While sluicing alluvial tin out the ground, Deny raised two daughters and campaigned for the area to be protected. Today's world heritage listing can be credited to his hospitality and persistent lobbying. We explored Deny's Kingdom in four wonderful weeks.

Moving closer to Hobart, Australia's second oldest city, we watched local boaties set gill nests and knew why we had trouble catching fish! Alongside Constitution Dock, where the Sydney Hobart racers tie up, was a special treat. Four lanes of capital city traffic at our doorstep meant every attraction lay just footsteps away.

A voyage around such a diverse continent as Australia is to journey through countless events, dangers, and images of beauty far beyond what can be illuminated in such a brief version.

For the full story, we suggest reading our first book, "Two's a Crew."

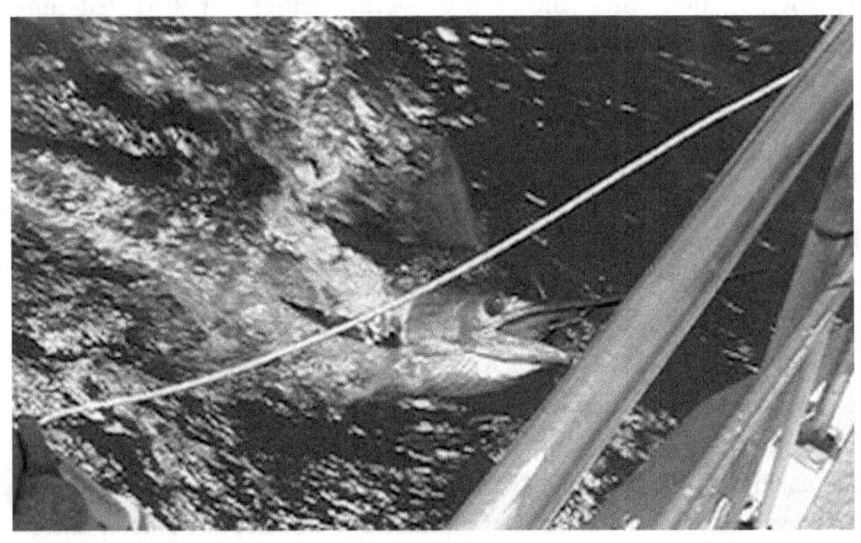

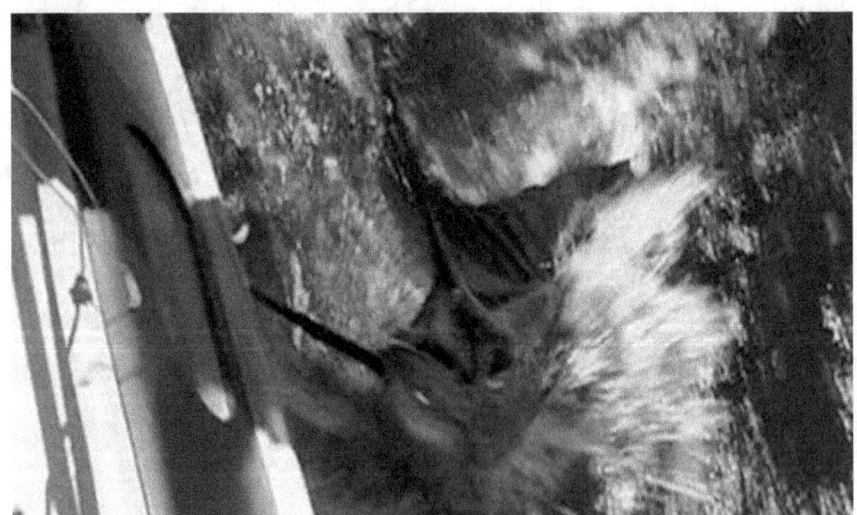

The moment of release

FISHING FOR MONSTERS

Walking aft I saw our Ocky strap bowstring tight and the trolling line singing. Shocked and alarmed, I jumped back shouting, "Hey Jude! Come look. Something huge is hooked up."

We nearly always troll a fishing lure when sailing during daylight hours. In the long ago past, we used to also dragged them during the night. But too many lures got taken by Noahs even after we devised a simple alarm consisting of an empty tin that fell to the deck whenever we had a strike. Whether then or now our setup has always been a simple handline. Attach the lure by a few metres of wire trace to a swivel then 50 m of 100 kg tested monofilament that's attached by another swivel to nearly 100 m of small-diameter braided sash cord that makes the initial haul-in a little easier on our hands. The boat end is attached to a strong Ocky strap held in a bight of line that only lets the strap stretch to a maximum length without breaking. Seeing how far it stretches is something like watching it weigh the fish. A normal-sized fish usually just takes the catenary out the line, but on this bright Sunday morn motoring over some of the world's best fishing ground, it was like a guitar string. We had just hooked a monster.

We didn't go near it. Any second something could snap and flick back into an eye.

"It's stretched tighter than when we hooked that fertiliser sack." I reminded Jude of the time we hooked a big woven plastic fertiliser bag that nearly stopped our boat when it popped open underwater. Just to be sure it wasn't another bag, I cautiously approached the line and tested its tautness then tiptoed back saying, "It's a real monster. Let's drag it for awhile and hope it gets free."

So we did just that with the white cord a tightrope you could walk on. For the next couple of miles we took turns searching the sea with the binoculars, but the sparkling sea hid our monster. Then in the briefest second, it suddenly rose close enough to the surface for me to see a long, sleek, dark body and long bill, which sent me racing for our video camera and calling, "It's a marlin or sailfish!"

Once when leaving the Cocos Keeling Islands with a similar fishing rig we hooked a two or three hundred kilo black marlin. In those days *Banyandah* had two masts and we attached the trolling line to the smaller mast's support wires. But we stopped doing that after the black marlin nearly pulled it over. These days we attach the trolling gear to our new stout aft tower.

For a good twenty minutes the video recorded a rather boring scene of blue sea and bowstring tight line, which eventually had me giving it a few serious jerks to wake the fellow up. But whoever was on the line was happy to tag-along, sometimes racing to one side and then the other. Not once did it jump free of the sea, so we shut down the recorder and simply waited. And so did our monster, for another good hour. Completely bored now, I took matters in hand. Damn! I hate getting sucked into battling big fish.

Jude was assigned the all-important task of head camerawoman in addition to her regular duty, which is to keep the gathered line away from my body in case the beast makes a run that I can't turn. With a serious face, she uttered a few words of encouragement then followed that up with a stern warning to be careful. Nodding that I would, I took hold of the braided sash cord and started hauling. Once started, I try to keep it coming. Slacken off and the beast might turn and run. The idea is to force the creature up to the surface where its powerful tail is less efficient. Steadily, hand over hand using the strength in my back and arms I pulled, all the time dreading the beast might run. But it didn't. So I kept yelling, "Come on. Tail-walk you crazy fish. Throw the hook."

When just a boat length astern, this most magnificent creature was seen gliding effortlessly through the water with its iridescent blue sail fully extended. And when almost close enough to touch, the creature finally jumped out the water like an excited puppy on a short leash. That's when its flashing tail splashed the sea's surface and its noble head shook in a last ditch effort to throw the lure. Oh, how we wished to see it flung free. But we didn't, and the beast fell back exhausted, to be towed on its side while we wondered what to do next.

"Put that camera down, now!" I ordered Jude, no longer able to keep the worry out my voice. "Get the biggest pliers quick!" Meanwhile my eyes were glued on the beast, expecting any moment to see it come alive and take a run. Instead, our eyes made contact and our minds interacted,

Fishing for Monsters

and in my head I'm sure I heard it say it would wait. Jude returned with my water pump pliers, and without hesitation, I leant over the rail and grabbed the bugger by his sword. God! He was as big as me and so much more powerful. But looking again into its eyes, I think this guy had been through this before. He was staring at me and seemed to be saying, "Okay, let's get this over. Stick your tag into me and I'll be on my way." Fine by me. A cooperative beast. Sure made my job of reaching into its jaws with the pliers and twisting out the hook a whole lot easier. After checking that Jude had the camera whirling, I released its sword and was delighted to see a huge splash, and with a quick swish of its tail, the creature flashed away.

We had had lots of excitement, plenty of photos, but no fish. So Jude convinced me to put the lure out again. I must have rocks in my head because an hour later we had the same scenario. Another taut line dragging a very boisterous critter that was a fair bit smaller. Nevertheless, we dragged it for half an hour because I was still recovering from the last battle. Eventually there was another hand-over-hand tussle, this time a shiny, slippery, stinky barracuda hit the deck. It's a fish we absolutely hate. This one broke free, went berserk snapping its dagger teeth and leaving a slimy trail over the side.

Now Jude, she's a vixen. She put on her prettiest face, cuddled me, massaged my drooping arms, and, well, I put the lure out a third time. Fortunately, nothing happened. Not straight away. Not till about four when the sun was heading for Africa did we hear the plastic spool clunk against the tower. I let out a moan, feeling decidedly weaker. I would have settled for a steaming bowl of pasta, but being a good sailor boy and a slave to my lady, I took up my station back aft and tested the line. You know, you can feel the brute shake its head when trying to throw the hook, and feeling that sent adrenalin through me. A fight hey! You want to take me on? Okay, try it. So I pulled. And it fought. And I pulled some more using my shoulders and the strength in my back, which was about all I had left. Fifteen minutes later, the bell rang ending round ten and a 20 kg wahoo was heaved alongside where Jude ripped into it with the gaff. The two of us then struggled to bring a wiggling monster up over the railing. All of a sudden, we had more fish then we could eat in a week. And that called for a cold beer before the bigger job of carving it up.

Australia Day at Fremantle Sailing Club

THE PEOPLE YOU MEET

When we were guests of the Fremantle Sailing Club, I awoke feeling a bit old this particular morning. Too much booze or one too many stories the night before had me feeling every one of my sixty-four years and I was crawling rather lethargically round the cabin when I heard a rap on our railing. Coming up my eyes clasped onto a man my age inspecting my boat.

"Bonny wee sailing ship you have laddie," were his first words, and I smiled. I love people who like my boat, and replied, "She's stout and looks after you in a storm and that's what matters, plus she's a treat to live aboard."

"Aye, I can see that," this fellow went on, his bushy eyebrows going up and down as he ran his eye over our craft.

"You're a Scot, I can tell. My wife's a Geordie." And with that disclosure, he ambled closer.

"Aye, a bonny lad from the old country." He said when we were eyeball to eyeball.

"Been back lately?" I asked, thinking of our own trip home to England in 1999.

"Aye. Went back in 2005."

"Good flight?"

"Did nay fly, I sailed."

"You sailed back to Scotland!" I exclaimed suddenly reassessing this man. I had been more concerned with my own problems that morning as we'd been meeting so many other folk full of dreams and claims.

Curious I asked, "Did you do the Red Sea and canal?" Thinking what a silly question, but having twice traversed the Red Sea, thought I'd hear the latest.

But what I next heard wiped away every remaining concern for my aging.

"No, didn't do the canal. We rounded the Horn."

"What! You went round the Horn! How big a boat?

"33 feet."

"And how many souls on board?"

"Just me."

"Oh you've got to be kidding, you sailed solo round the horn, and… and you must be my age." I hesitated over the last not wanting to ruffle his feathers.

"Aye and maybe I've a few years on you. I first rounded the Horn when I was seventy. Rounded it again when I turned seventy five, and if my bonnie lassie will let me out again, I'll round it again in two years time when I'm eighty."

Somehow I knew this man was genuine, so I said nothing but slid my hand across the rail to encompass his. Looking into those warm gentle eyes, I felt the man's lust for life pour through me and suddenly I was not the least concerned that I was 4,000 miles from my home and about to turn a mere sixty-five.

Later that same morning, when the club's bosun bid me good day and I called him to the rail to disclose what I'd heard. He smirked and commented, "Oh so you've met George. Last time he rounded the Horn, he had to go aloft to fix a parted halyard and slipped and fell. His foot caught in a step loop and ripped some tendons. But George just got himself down the mast, bandaged his leg then carried on round the Horn non stop to Scotland."

Well, since meeting George, I have never once felt the advancing years blues. And when alone on a dark watch I feel the man beside me, and together we puff out our chests, happy to still sail the sea, and with pride we look out over the inky blackness to the stars

The People You Meet

Our first book
One of the world's greatest adventures
following Flinders wake around Australia
9,000 nautical miles across six climatic zones

Alongside Emu Point Slipway the two Jacks taking the salt air

LATE NIGHT VISITOR

Asleep one night while *Banyandah* was moored alongside the Emu Point Slipway in Albany, I heard my darling lady shouting, "Put that down. Get out of it."

Groggy, coming out a deep sleep, I thought she was dreaming and was about to comfort her when I felt her crawl over me. I sleep closest to the companionway, so that got me wide awake.

Rising in the dim light, I heard Jude shout that someone had been on our boat and had just gotten off. So without a thought, I was away like a shot, over the handrail, onto the dock and off towards the empty parking lot. In the single arc lamp, a large figure was stealing off with something in his arms. I ran after, shouting, "Put that stuff down! Walk away and nothing more will happen!"

Reaching alongside the figure, he was bigger than me, shirtless and carrying our two green shopping bags in one hand, and in the other, swishing round n'round something like a long Kung Fu stick, which I carefully kept out of its range.

"Now look buddy, you don't want any trouble. Just put that stuff down and get out of here, and there'll be no trouble." Not a word in reply, just the swishing of that long stick. I looked about the dark marina, not a soul in sight. Looking back to the young man, the stick flashed through the arc light and became our homemade boat hook, its sharp stainless end doubles as a gaff.

Jude now suddenly rushed up and damn near tackled the fellow, and I had to yell at her, "Keep away. He's got our boat hook!"

In a shrill voice she yelled out, "That's my dirty laundry in those bags! Just put it down and get out of here."

What was this character doing? Dead of night, stealing dirty laundry and an ancient boathook. I didn't want trouble, not for us nor this young fellow. But he wouldn't stop walking towards the exit, so I began screaming out "Help! Help!" Robber! Help!" I was so loud; someone would either come running or call the police. But the lad just kept slopping along the payment and no one came to our aid.

Emu Point Slipway is an industrial area. There's a marina, but few people are there at night. "Look lad, my lady and I built that boat, we built every scrap of her then sailed around the world, raising our children afloat. So she's precious to us. Won't you just put the stuff down and walk away. I promise there'll be no further trouble."

And just about when I'd given up all hope, he stopped. And then slowly put the bags and hook down. Then shuddering, he began to cry.

The world's a tough place. And having pulled myself out from a rather horrible start, I find time for lost souls wherever I encounter them.

Reaching up, putting my arm around his bare shoulder, I comforted him and asked what was the matter?

In a torrent, outpoured, "They mistreat me. Won't let me out. Don't understand."

Jude picked up the laundry and moved the boathook away from the two of us while I asked, "Are you talking about your family?"

"No, I've been in hospital, but the nurse abuses me, so tonight I ran away. I didn't mean any trouble. Just thought I could get some money to get to my dad."

I was still just in my nightshirt and suddenly feeling the cold said, "Look, why don't we go back to the boat. Are you hungry?"

Well, of course we didn't get on the *Banyandah*, but sat on the dock alongside her, and while Jude made us cups of tea and slices of bread with marmalade, I listened to this young lads outpouring.

In a nutshell, he wasn't crazy. Just knew his rights, as we all do with the tellie informing us all the time that we have the right to this or that. And he'd found an easy way through life as a ward of our great nation. At the present moment, he was checked into a mental hospital claiming he had self-harm problems, and oh yeah, he'd been abused.

I grew up in LA. The world's most fierce city. Walk into a payphone and the sharp edge of a knife might find your throat. Park your car on a dark street and a pistol may greet your exit. Abused? Crikey, I got touched up at thirteen and was drugged by two old farts at eighteen. So I told this young man there's no profit in looking back. Life is the future, not the past. It's tough enough without carrying extra baggage. Then thinking of our welfare system, I asked, "What's the matter, you don't like hard work?"

"No, I don't mind working. My dad and I once picked fruit and I enjoyed lugging around the bins."

"Well then, Life is an opportunity. Get off your butt and go somewhere in life. The system will make you a captive. They only pay you enough to survive, but not to progress. And unless you make a break, you'll be no more than you are now for the rest of your life. Look at us; we've seen the world, love all critters, and are still going strong because we have dreams."

Yes, I know, that philosophy won't erase a lifetime of problems in a couple of hours, so we asked if he had family then listen to a string of woes about broken marriages and his mom's new man not wanting him around. It didn't surpass my own history.

"What about your dad?"

"Yeah, he's great. In Queensland but..."

"Well, that seems the best course to me. Change of venue gives you a new start, and if your dad will help, you'll have some support while you get yourself moving forward again. Just find a dream."

Considering it was three in the morning, Jude then asked the most important question, "What are you going to do now?"

"Dunno."

Always practical she suggested, "Why not go back to the hospital and tell them what you've done and ask them to place a telephone call to your father."

Surprising us both, he agreed, so we gave him a shirt and old jumper, exchanged my Ugg boots he'd nicked for a pair of sunny Queensland flip-flops, and he walked out of our lives.

Jude called the hospital around ten the next morning, and the staff nurse exclaimed, "Oh, you're the couple." Then she reported that he'd told her the whole story and that they were attempting to put him in touch with his father. Do hope his life has a happy ending. A few days after that we set sail off across the Great Australian Bight.

Reflections in a Sailor's Eyes

Waychinicup - the locals swear it is safe
But that's the Southern Ocean just outside the narrow crack.

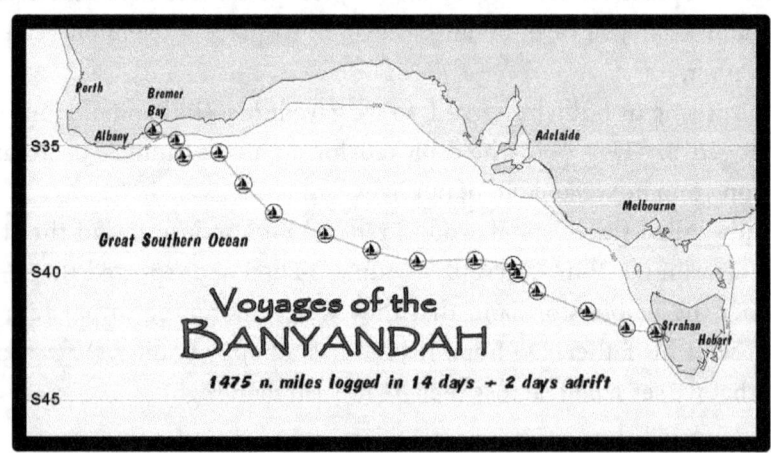

MOONLIGHT ACROSS THE SOUTHERN OCEAN

By the time the Roaring Forties pass under Australia, they have gathered energy from halfway around Earth and are either driving the sea wild or are ready to pounce when next provoked by a depression from Antarctica.

Now imagine two aging flower powers, petals shrivelling yet with bright strong hearts, aboard a homemade sailboat crossing this much feared stretch of water. Alone, they must look after themselves and God forbid either be injured or suffer a body malfunction.

With my eyes aglow I have told others about the time we made a winter crossing from Albany to Wilson Promontory, me on the aft deck cudgelling the heavens trying to match Nature's fury as a black front passes overhead. With that glow replaced by humble respect, I then describe how *Banyandah* began lifting to a wave that soared high above her masthead. When its top third tumbled and turned white, froth flew from its crest, and roaring like a fast train, chased *Banyandah* down till it washed over us.

Once Again

Eighteen months ago, with little thought of the dangers and difficulties, the *Two J's* took on this challenge once again. At that time *Banyandah* rested peacefully between two towering red cliffs of the Berkeley River gorge, a slender slit in the arid Western Australia landscape. Sitting in the shade of her awning we were listening to Matt and Gill relive again their adventures aboard *Wooshee* when surrounded by thick Tasmanian rainforest of the mighty Gordon River. We love those ancient silent monsters with branches dripping green mosses, so the thought of living among such grandeur had us put that destination on our must do list while circumnavigating Australia.

But making a promise is one thing, fulfilling it another. Especially when it involves crossing 1600 nm of the Roaring Forties and then making landfall on a lee shore that has only one safe haven, and it guarded by a narrow gap called Hells Gate.

Months of voyaging and other activities had distracted our thoughts until we began our road trip back to *Banyandah*, left in Albany during an east coast winter's break visiting family. In a lifetime of tackling challenges we have found good preparations lay the foundation to success. With this in mind, we had returned with two new sails and a new safety device that sounds an alarm should the watch keeper fall overboard while the other is sleeping.

By November we were back at Emu Point Slipway where *Banyandah* stood forlorn like a warrior in tarnished armour awaiting some care. Here we received the best assistance from Darren Russell, a journeyman shipwright and owner of the friendliest slipway in Australia.

Waiting for the Moon

Six weeks of steady work had our good ship ready for sea, but we hung around for the new moon's slender face as there's nothing quite as grand as sailing an empty sea bathed in moonlight. Two days before Christmas, we cast free our lines and sailed straight into a near gale, thinking if something's going to bust, best it happens close to facilities. Sailors don't have public holidays; everyone knows that. So while most were ripping open gifts, our Christmas Day was celebrated by having one of our loveliest sails within cooee of gigantic granite boulders, washed and weathered by white breakers off a sapphire sea.

We gunk-holed along the south coast while trying to find our sea legs again, sleeping well at Two-Peoples Bay, Waychinicup, and Cape Riche. But the night before our departure we slept poorly. Not from nerves, but from a nasty Southern Ocean swell rolling into Bremer Bay. I swore a blue streak all night that continued well into the morning as we packed our disaster grab bag and lashed emergency provisions into the *Little Red*, our tinny. In a more positive note, we both slept well our first night at sea when usually it takes a few nights before we become so fatigued we don't hear the groans, clicks, and sea sounds that stops sleep coming easily.

Moonlight Across the Southern Ocean

Whispering Easterlies

Leaving with no malicious weather approaching, our first challenge was finding a way through the prevailing summer high pressure cell which contained only whispering easterly headwinds. With the rig in tight, we sailed full and by, increasing the apparent wind which increased our speed to slightly faster than if walking upon that mirror flat ocean. Southing came slowly those first five days while our watch keeping settled into a rhythm. Jude retired at eight, but not before seeing that I'd clipped on our watch keeper's belt containing personal EPIRB, waterproof strobe, whistle, and a small transmitter that activates an onboard siren if the wearer should fall overboard.

We always post a watch. No exceptions. Dangers materialise when least expected. So, regular as clockwork, at 15 minutes past midnight I wake Jude. Then, if needed, we make any sail changes. This helps me sleep till the eastern horizon lightens. Often, I slip into a bed still warm from my lady's sleep. In the past we have tried shifts of two, three, and four-hours. But I took so long to fall asleep that now we simply split the night in two. Jude takes a morning nap to gain extra rest.

Strengthening Westerlies

Slow, easy miles slid past until one morning a band of cloud wet our decks. Then presto, like an ace thumped down on a jack, the wind magically swung to the west. At last the sails could be eased, although running from rather light winds actually slowed our progress. But with each passing day, as the moon grew larger, so did the wind strength until when celebrating one week at sea, it came in strong, forcing us to reef down for the first time. Barrelling along at double pace, *Banyandah* rolled heavily in the increased swell. Tossed one way then the other, sleeping fitfully, I cursed the sudden repetitive squeaking of a windvane block until I could stand it no more. Boldly braving a wetting, I clambered topsides, braced my bum on the wet aft deck, clamped a torch between my teeth, and then tried to lubricate the offending block. Alas, all in vain. Towelling the cold sea off my torso, shivering, I climbed back into bed. Moments later I was shoving tissues into my ears in a futile effort to silence the persistent squeal that was still driving me insane. Those 24 hours were our greatest run. One hundred and forty-three nautical miles logged. Not our greatest ever, which is nearer two hundred, but a good day's run nonetheless.

Filled with Nature

You might think mid-ocean a boring lonely place, but it's not. A long voyage like this becomes an intimate passage through time and space filled with Nature. Seabirds kept us company, clouds whisked overhead, and sea swells passed in ever-changing patterns. Early on, flocks of brown mutton birds swooped down behind us after we'd landed a big fish. Greedily they dove deep to retrieve chunks we threw them, using their wings to fly under the sea like cormorants. And if they missed, atop the sea they'd beat their wings and paddle their feet to chase *Banyandah*.

Further south, when the breeze acquired a real bite, giant albatross soared gracefully astern, effortlessly travelling many miles without moving their three-metre wings. Surely, man's first gliders were fashioned after them. Some had black slashes like mascara running through their eyes, others had snow white wings edged in the deepest black, and a few had patterned bodies like fine Italian marble. Other creatures were about too. Shearwaters soared swiftly along the swells, and tiny storm petrels no bigger than would fit in our hands, their pink legs dangling, danced from wave top to wave top searching for food among the breaking seas hundreds of miles from land. These creatures of mid-ocean survive in all winds. In fact, the more it blows, the faster they swoop and soar, seeming to enjoy the extra power and challenge as they race one another in magnificent displays of aerobatics.

Keeping a Log

We keep a log of our journey. Each hour of every day, we record the cumulative miles *Banyandah* has run, course steered, miles achieved, wind speed and direction, barometric pressure, plus any notes we like to make. Sound like a chore? Not a bit. In fact, when the ship's bell strikes the hour we relish the opportunity to record our passage. It'd be more than 30 years since we started with store-bought logbooks, which soon proved rather expensive, so we designed our own that also contained a form for reducing sextant sights and noon meridian passages. We recorded thousands of sea miles using these photocopies mounted in folders, then had a 300 page hardback book printed for peanuts in Sri

Lanka. Today we use lined A4 hardback notebooks obtainable from most newsagents that Jude rules into columns. She also beautifully embellishes the pages with creatures we see, while all I can muster are doodles of our sail plan. With additional comments, some humorous, some laconic, a few distressed, they form an informative record of journeys we never want to forget.

Strong Winds

When sailing south of latitude forty, strong winds came more frequently and we listened intently to the high seas weather forecasts issued four hourly by the Bureau of Meteorology on frequency 8176. Recording the huge amount of data first on an MP3 recorder, we then replayed it until we could graph the highs, fronts, and depressions. At those latitudes, the weather changes quickly. And when, just two days from landfall, a deep 970 mb low developed astern, instead of finding sleep, my mind gnawed on whether to divert to a more northern harbour or try to survive hove-to in strong gale conditions. We were checking into the Seafarer's Amateur Radio Net, reporting our position and weather, so I asked if they would check out the anchorage on King Island as an alternative. But the next day, when that depression got pushed further south and our area would receive only the cold front and 30 knots, we maintained our course.

Tasmania

Our first sight of Tasmania came soon after that cold front had given us a kick up the backside. Seen between crashing waves, the mountain peaks sent our hearts soaring with pride and relief. By noon we were as close as we dared, just eight miles offshore. It was too late to attempt an entry so we rolled up the headsail, pulled the main in tight and hove-to. As if waiting for us to arrive, the wind eased and King Neptune's welcoming committee leapt out the sea to race past our bows in the largest pod of dolphins seen since our earliest passages.

The lessening breeze tempted us to make a dash for the dreaded narrow gap of Hells Gate, but we resisted. Later, as the horizon darkened for yet another night at sea and the wind evaporated, I questioned if I'd made the right decision. Jude bedded down, and as we were back in mobile phone range, I settled into answering our inbox. However, the wind gods weren't done with us yet. While bobbing up and down with a dark hostile coastline now only five miles to our lee, the wind roared back with a vengeance not seen on this passage. *Banyandah* shook and she rocked. The cacophony was so deafening, Jude roared out. "What's going on?"

Vexation showing, I roared back, "Get some sleep." Though I knew she could not.

Staying Awake

Hoping she'd get some rest, fearing she'd be clumsy if not, I tried to stay awake further into the night, but even the slatting sail and slosh of sea couldn't hold back my weariness. Droopy eyed and unable to stay awake any longer, just as I climbed into her warm bunk, the wind ceased as if the gods had shut off a tap. Shaking my head while pulling up the doona, the wind suddenly roared back – from the opposite direction!

All Quiet

Exhaustion must have blocked out all noise and violent motion for I woke only when soft shadows crept into the cabin. Stumbling up, rubbing sleepy eyes, I saw Jude sitting in her chartreuse down jacket, ghostly white, staring blankly across a misty sea. The wind had gone, the sea was quiet, and a quick check of the GPS showed Cape Sorell just three miles off. Gulping down a quick coffee, I started the diesel, and through the mist, *Banyandah* went toward her destination.

Jude didn't go back to bed. With land getting nearer her cheeks found their normal blush and she eagerly grabbed her camera. Sea-mist swirled like steam and first sight through the eerie light came the lonely white edifice of the Cape Sorell lighthouse atop ravaged rocks as *Banyandah* rode the Great Southern Ocean swell on to her next challenge.

Not that long ago, in January 1822, two British ships set out from Hobart with orders to establish a place of banishment, *'to put the fear of God and Hell into the most incorrigible of Van Diemens Land prisoners.'* Only one, the *Sophia*, successfully navigated through the narrow gap into Macquarie Harbour. Landing at Sarah Island, Commandant Cuthbertson, his officials and a detachment of soldiers incarcerated 66 male and 8 female convicts in the most miserable place imaginable. The wretched souls passing through this narrow gap called it Hells Gate.

Free in spirit and commanding our own destinies, as we approached this treacherous gap the sun broke through bathing us in warmth that added life to the vibrant colours of forest meeting bold rocky shore. Just ahead lay an opening no larger than three houses abreast holding back a 50 km long body of water filled by the rivers draining southwest Tasmania.

Slack Water

More often than not, strong currents make this gap untenable and to enter at slack water was one reason we had waited. That strategy payed dividends because we had to battle against only a few knots with mild swirling eddies. While dancing round the deck recording the scenery on video we thought of those poor devils who had spent their last days in this wet lonely place. But instead of leading us into misery, that narrow gap magically opened into an unbelievable expanse of smooth water where, for the first time in weeks, *Banyandah* ceased rocking. To not have to brace our every step, to not be thrown against bulkheads and doorways immediately lifted a burden that sent our spirits soaring higher still.

When seeing the small town of Strahan appear around a headland came the realisation that we had achieved a dream held since that day with Matt and Gill. We had conquered the Great Southern Ocean. Before us now was the reality of a rainforest retreat. As well, another dream could now be achieved. To our south within easy reach lay the massive waterway of Port Davy; World Heritage, without tracks or roads. We'll be going there next, to explore and be amazed by the majesty of Earth.

Atop the King George River Falls

Dangerous ground throughout Kimberley

THE FALL OF NAN JUDE

During our first visit to the Kimberley we discovered a great love for those ancient rock paintings known as Bradshaws, thought to be the world's oldest art. Our fondest memories of that voyage are treks inland searching for new Bradshaw paintings, and therefore when planning a new journey across Australia's Top End, we pencilled in a week long search centred on the King George River where we'd previously found a great cache of art.

Leaving our home port of Ballina in June, we sailed through the wildlife rich Coral Sea then went past Thursday Island on strong easterlies to Darwin, logging close to 3000 miles with just a few touches of land.

In Darwin a week of hectic preparations saw us crossing the Joseph Bonaparte Gulf after little rest for we were in a hurry to begin our quest. Three days later, luck had us landfall at Gallery Bay with enough daylight to launch *Little Red* and search for the freshwater we'd seen on our first visit. It was important to find freshwater there as it would be our turnaround point. But when pushing through the thorny scrub under the caves filled with rock art, Jude staggered, and then sat down. "Gee, I feel giddy," she laughed. "Guess I haven't found my land legs yet."

The very next day, hardly an hour after anchoring in front of the Twin Falls on the King George River, we were climbing a steep rocky slope to gain a magnificent view over the red rock gorge with *Banyandah* looking minuscule amongst three multihull water beetles.

Although oppressively hot, we spent the day in training, walking several kilometres inland on the plateau above the falls, trying to adjust to the climate and terrain for the much longer walk we planned for a few days hence. Hot, sticky, our spirits sky-high but stamina low, we found a delicious freshwater pool and swam naked without fear of salty crocs mauling us. On our way home through the cooling landscape of red flowering eucalypts and yellow kapoks we dallied until approaching the top of the falls where the lengthening shadows painted the canyons with the flames of a great fire. Every crack, dark and sinister, down to a steel blue hearth upon which *Banyandah* lay surrounded by awesome beauty.

When stepping closer to the eroded edge for one last photo, the silence of faraway space was suddenly shattered. First by a dull thud then by such a cry as if an old mamma bear had caught a paw in a steel trap. After that one cry, the eerie stillness returned, punctuated by the barely perceptible whimpering of Jude calling my name.

Jude Relating How It Happened

Jack was out of sight when I stepped down off a rock ledge onto what I thought was low scrub a metre below. Trouble was I kept falling, my foot speared down a hole until it bottomed out with my thigh almost level with the ground. Through my body shot an electric shock that stunned me when I thought I heard bone breaking. Subconsciously in those first few seconds I'm rubbing my hands, grazed by their impact with rock as I tried to save myself. Then a wave of sickness hits and any wonder if it had been a bad dream vanishes.

But Jack was soon standing above me, ashen faced, haggard with concern, and picking green ants from my flesh which I vaguely felt biting me.

Next he's carefully easing me out the hole and away from the green ants now swarming over me. Then gently pulling up my trouser, he's examining my leg. I'm watching him do this, somewhat relieved. There's no sign of blood thank goodness! Or bones sticking out.

After the first wave of sickness subsided I demand the backpack he's pulled off me. After tipping its contents out, locate first aid kit, then immediately swallow four painkillers in one gulp. For support I'm then strapping my knee tightly with a strong five-inch crepe bandage knowing I'd need it. Thankfully we always carry good equipment whenever we leave *Banyandah*. Loving the wild places, we're always aware of our remoteness to help.

With the sun now only a finger width above the western ridge, the thought of what would come next figured high in both our minds. We didn't know if my leg was broken or just terribly sprained. But we did know, if we pushed the

The Fall of Nan Jude

red *rescue* button on our PLB, our floating home at the base of the King George River Falls would be left stranded. For how would we return? Say from Darwin, nearly a thousand kilometres away. There are no roads. Access is only by helicopter or ship.

"Let's see if you can stand," Jack repeated.

"Right," I nodded affirmatively, pretending to agree with him, but not really sure my leg or my will could do it. All I could think about was our Shattered Dream.

Our eyes met. I trusted him but still said, "I can't do it," almost bursting into tears. Jack didn't mince words. "Look girl, unless you want to spend the night in the open, probably making matters much worse, you've got to move." That put the fear into me. I moved, attempting to get up. Suddenly he's pulling me up, taking my weight with a shoulder and a hand under my armpits I got to standing. For an instant hope rose in me that my leg would come good. I'm also thinking that I must do this before the pain really kicks in.

Our first step was awkward. We almost tumbled the second. The third brought us to the offending rock ledge where Jack sat me down. It was dead obvious the sun would soon set. And I just longed to lie down until fear took over with Jack saying, "Look, we'll be out here all night unless we get our timing right. I'll call out the steps. You put your weight on me and do your best."

I get up. "Step," he urged and we hobble forward. Then I hear "step" again and see him pointing to an open spot. I obey. What else could I do? I'm no wimp, and he's puffing away with the exertion of hauling me along; anyways I was beginning to feel stupid. We've had our fair share of scary dramas - more than many in our life exploring Earth, and that has galvanised our partnership into 'we can do this' mentality.

We navigated down into the black rock riverbed and it was much cooler now that the sun had fallen below the ridgeline. Its flat surface made going easier until we were confronted by the bushy land rising up the other side. That bit was awkward. The big boulders and stouter trees stopped us going two abreast.

Jack was pretty knackered when we tried the descent. He went ahead and I tried leaning on his shoulders, but this was unsettling. I'm high above him and know if I toppled there'd be no way I could stop falling on my leg again.

Then when we nearly toppled over, I sat down proclaiming, "I'm going down on my bottom." And surprised myself with how well it went. Yes, huge pain now, but being on my bottom low to the ground I hadn't the added fear of falling again, and using my arms and one good leg, rock by rock, some nearly my height, I practically slid down the slope. Jack fetched the dinghy to an easier place and while I waited my left leg throbbed, feeling ready to explode.

In the last shred of light I demanded to row us home, to take my mind off the pain. Upon reaching *Banyandah* we spent several minutes figuring out how to get me aboard. Which position in the dinghy was easiest to get out from? Not liking the idea of being hoisted up by a halyard, I ended up gripping the handrails and pulling my weight up then dropping my bum on the side deck, all with Jack's help.

Now some things happen for a reason. To not lose our fresh veggies when we went away for our weeks walk, as a trial we'd left the fridge cycling on and off, not our normal routine. So good fortune found me cold packing my very swollen leg with cans of beer, and swallowing several more painkillers and a couple of anti-inflammatory tablets.

That night Jack went a bit overboard on red wine and fell asleep in the cockpit. Can't say I blame him. My brain was so drugged up too, fantasising springing from bed next morning just a tad black and blue and asking which day would we start our big trek. Alas, reality is not so forgiving.

Jack Continues

In the morning, Judith couldn't move her leg. It was yellow and blue, puffed up, skin stretched tightly, her knee hugely swollen, and her ankle one great puffball. The good news was she could wiggle her toes and just move her ankle. She continued the anti-inflammatory drugs and spent the day in bed. By nightfall she could flex her knee and we celebrated.

After three days with little more improvement the cruise ship *True North* eased past to reach the falls, and I called to ask if they had a doctor on board, explaining Jude's injury.

The Fall of Nan Jude

Miraculously within thirty minutes a workboat came alongside carrying a doctor on holiday from NZ, a bright cheery lady who just happened to be an orthopaedic surgeon! After an examination in our cockpit, the doctor told us she could not rule out a fracture of the tibia or ligament damage, but she felt both were unlikely because Judith had mobility and had recovered so quickly. We then discussed our options. Considering our remote location, she said no further damage would be done if Judith continued to rest, and when the swelling went down, she agreed we could sail to a location for x-rays and diagnoses. Jude, knowing the doctor came from a small country, mentioned that further treatment might be four, even six weeks away. The doctor reassured us, "If it's fractured, it can always be reset later." Her visit gave us both peace of mind and the information to make a decision. Thank you Margaret and thank you *True North*.

For two long windless weeks we idled within the confines of the river, me in bed taking pills and feeling miserable while Jack edited video. Then the mechanical weather forecaster uttered those miraculous words, "Strengthening east winds in the north Kimberley." Still unable to walk, my ankle still a puff ball, my knee unable to take weight, and both of us wondering how I'd survive the jostling of *Banyandah*, nevertheless we departed. Jack had already mastered loading the tinny and outboard alone, but wasn't sure how he'd manage the ship without me. Once clear of the islands and reefs entrapping us, we planned to keep going even if we drifted. Like Jack said, what couldn't we do floating in a bug free ocean that we did when anchored amongst crocs and midges?

Our first day went easily for me. I hardly moved. Moving around was too painful, as was swinging myself through the boat using the handholds which are in every deck-frame. So all day I stayed braced in the corner of the cockpit with my knee bent over a large cushion while Jack looked after me and our ship. The only time I moved was to use a handy bucket. We cleared all dangers before sunset in an exciting day's run beating currents around islands and avoiding two very curious humpback whales that kept pace then charged alongside causing a few adrenalin rushes. All while we're flying along with a sweet 15 knots filling our sails.

Instead of changing watch at midnight, Jack didn't nudge me awake to take mine until nearly 3 AM. Then he's up again at first light resetting the sails and making us breakfast. With only one good leg to stand on it was impossible for me to be in the galley underway; one hand had to hold on, and my hip braced hard against the cupboard front already bruised from just light boat movements.

By midnight day three we were adrift. Jack rolled in the headsail, pulled the main in tight then put me in charge while he went below for a well-earned sleep.

Judith looked like cold toast when I arose from the aft cabin, so I sent her to bed even before surveying the calm expanse of blue sea. The bureau forecast a few windless days, so I turned to the chart and discovered, a mere 20 miles further on lay Adele Reef. Our WA Cruising Guide didn't mention Adele, so I dug out our rather old Australian Pilot and was surprised by it stating that Adele had a superb anchorage which should be entered at low water. Checking the tides, we could be there just about then, so I fired up the iron topsail and off we went across the flat sea.

Adele Reef lies some 50 miles north of Cape Leveque and King Sound, and measures 6 miles by 13 miles north to south. It doesn't have a navigable lagoon, but rather an inlet created where the reef nicks in several miles on its eastern side. The chart also shows a couple of sand islands, one rather sizable with a light.

It was roasting hot by the time we arrived off Fraser Inlet and Jack and I were quite ready for a rest after an instrument failure caused a comical drama on arrival. The Adele anchorage was perfect for me. Super calm, easy for me to get around the boat. And what an amazing sight. A mass of sand. But which two bits were the islands?

I could hardly wait to get off the boat and into the water as I was hoping the aqua therapy would improve my leg. Just to float and be able to take the weight off my body was my dream after three weeks 'bottom bound'. The following day when the tide was up we found a way through the shallows, scaring schools of fish on our way to the smaller cay. Jack ran the dinghy bow into its steep side then held it steady while I precariously crawled over the gunwale into the water. Then using an axe handle for a crutch I could only make it up the sloping sand a few metres. Close to tears I sat down, not an easy thing to do, but rather fortunately I had planted myself within metres of a brown-booby sitting on an egg. Left alone while Jack went off beach-combing, at least I could tell that bird my woes. I knew, after almost three weeks gone, I had done serious damage to my leg. Still feeling sorry for myself, I crawled back to the water's edge and rolled in. Oh! What heavenly bliss, a weightless feeling, the water up to my chest, cooling my leg, helping the swelling. I felt renewed. It was great bobbing along the smooth sandy bottom on my good leg while exercising my very tired arm muscles.

Every day at Adele we repeated this. Trolling each day and within minutes of leaving the cay coming home we always caught a fish from those teeming around us. Enough for us and the crabs and other critters keeping the place so clean around us.

Leaving Adele Reef, a slow eight-day sail to Dampier, turned over five weeks since my accident. The Hampton Harbour Yacht Club loaned us a ute the next morning and we drove to the Nickol Bay Hospital at Karratha. We had to wait seven hours to be seen; but fair enough; five weeks getting to emergency meant I was at the bottom of the triage.

Unable to read the x-ray the emergency room doctor called the visiting orthopaedic surgeon, who by sheer good fortune was there that day. He's there only a few times a month.

The x-ray showed that when I fell forward the side ligaments did not snap. Instead, they held the knee together, so my femur crushed the top of my shinbone. A grandmother to eight I have some osteoporosis, i.e. soft bones, and so the outside of my knee joint was depressed approximately 1 cm, meaning my left leg is now unstable.

"How soon will I heal?" I asked the surgeon, and disturbed by his curt reply, I elaborated on what I do. "I go bushwalking – often. Even with the grandkids when we're home."

"Well. You'll not be doing any more of that," he told me in a stern gruff tone. "You'll not be able to walk on uneven ground again. Might as well give that idea up."

Well, not all doctors get it right. Sure the knee wobbles a bit, but there's no pain even when tramping through the bush if I use my walking stick. Personally I like what Margaret, the NZ surgeon recently wrote in an email: *At the end of the day if it is behaving itself reasonably and you are getting about to your satisfaction without having to limit yourself too badly, you carry on as usual.*

That sounds good advice and very thankfully, so far, we're getting along very well indeed.

Reflections in a Sailor's Eyes

Glossary

Aback: The wind is on the wrong side of the sails. Sometimes done deliberately to slow the speed.

Abeam: At right angles to the boat's centreline.

Aft: Towards or at the stern of the boat.

Antifouling: A specially formulated paint for coating a boat beneath the waterline to prevent growth of weed and barnacles.

Autopilot: An electric steering device that turns the rudder either via the steering wheel or directly.

Athwartships: Across a ship from side to side.

Beat: To sail as close as possible to the wind.

Beating to windward: Means tacking up wind.

Bilge, bilges: The lowest most internal part of the boat's hull used as a sump to drain any water which may have collected in the boat.

Bloke: a man

Bloody: very (bloody hard yakka)

Boom: Spar that runs horizontally to hold out the bottom of the mainsail.

Bow: Towards or at the front of a boat.

Bulkhead: Vertical partition usually installed to divide a vessel into cabins, and/or watertight compartments. Some bulkheads are for rigidity of construction.

Chainplates: Metal fittings on the sides and stern of a boat to which are fastened the standing rigging or shrouds.

Clew: After lower corner of a fore-and-aft sail..

Cockpit: Central lowered area between the forward living area and the aft cabin, where the helm and compass are.

Companionway: Opening and ladder leading from below decks to above decks.

Cooee: Nearby, I was within cooee of landing a big fish when the line broke.

Dodger: The solid structure over the forepart of the cockpit that protects the helmsman and companionway from the weather.

Fit-out: The built in interior of the boat.

Foredeck: The area of deck forward of the cockpit.

Forward: The front part of a vessel, at or near the bow.

Forestay: Rigging stay which runs from the stemhead on the bow to high on the mast. The headsails or jibs are set from the forestay.

Furling Headsail: Headsail set on an aluminium (foil) tube. This tube encases the forestay and the sail is stowed by rolling it around the foil.

Gooseneck fitting: Metal fitting at the forward end of the boom that attaches it to the mast, allowing the boom to turn in any direction.

Gybe: Turning a sailing vessel so that the wind passes from one side to the other across the stern.

Halyard: A rope, wire or wire-rope combination used for hoisting and lowering sails and flags on a mast.

Head: Toilet area in a vessel.

Keel: The fore-and-aft protruding fin under a vessel. The keel provides stability and stops sideways drift.

Knockdown A knockdown is the term used when a yacht is rolled over with her masts and sails in the water – usually in violent squalls or huge breaking seas.

Lead: The direction taken by a rope or sheet. Lead blocks are used to alter the direction.

Log: Ship's journal, in which all references to weather, navigation, and daily happenings aboard are recorded. Also a short version of 'sumlog': the device for measuring a boat's speed and distance travelled.

Loom: To appear in view indistinctly. Loom in the clouds is light reflected from a source below.

Luff: Forward edge if a fore-and-aft sail. The luff of the mainsail is the leading edge that runs up the mast.

On the nose: The wind comes from the direction in which one wants to sail. Beating to windward when the wind is on the nose.

Portholes: The windows in a vessel.

Reach: To sail on all points of the wind except running square.

Reef: To reduce sail area by folding (slab), rolling or lashing up sections of the sails. *Banyandah* has a roller-reefing headsail on the furling foil, and a slab-reefing mainsail.

Rhumb line: A direct line between two points.

Roller furler: Rotating foil and drum, usually over a forestay, for the headsail to roll and furl around.

Rudderpost or stock: Shaft to which the rudder is attached.

Running square: Sailing with the wind directly from behind.

Running rigging: The ropes used to control the sails.

Sextant: Navigation instrument which measures the angles of heavenly bodies in relation to the horizon.

Sheets: Lines or ropes attached to and used to trim or control the sails.

Sheila: a woman

Skeg: Metal or timber support for a rudderpost.

Slipped: To slip a vessel is to haul it out of the water for repairs, modification, or antifouling treatment.

Sole: Floor of the cabin in a yacht.

Stem: The stem is the curved part of the boat at the bow into which the side parts of the boat run. The stemhead is the top of this structure at deck level.

Stern: Furthest aft part of a vessel.

Stern gland: Gland where the propeller shaft runs through the hull. The stern gland is usually packed with greasy hemp so that the shaft can turn but water cannot enter the hull.

Standing rigging: The wires supporting the masts.

Sumlog: Device to measure a vessel's speed and distance travelled.

Swages: Metal bands or collars that are slipped over two wires and then crimped with a special tool so that the wires are joined together.

Tacking: To bring vessel into wind then take wind on the other side.

Tinny: small aluminium boat

Top End: Far north of Australia

Transom: The back of the hull, running across the stern.

Ute: utility vehicle, pickup truck

Windvane: A mechanical device that steers a yacht in a direction in relationship to the wind. *Banyandah* has its own small rudder (servo) attached by lines to the steering tiller.

Yakka: Work (noun), as in hard yakka.

www.ingramcontent.com/pod-product-compliance
Lightning Source LLC
Chambersburg PA
CBHW050637300426
44112CB00012B/1833